The Secrets of Jerusalem

Tzvia Dobrish-Fried

The Secrets of Jerusalem

Tzvia Dobrish-Fried

Photographs: Uriel Messa

 MODAN PUBLISHING HOUSE

THE SECRETS OF JERUSALEM
Tzvia Dobrish-Fried

English: Barry Davis
Graphic design: Studio Rotem: Ada Vardi

Dedicated with love to
my parents
Fani and Tinu Dobrish

Contents

Foreword: The Secret of the Stones

There are cities of the sea, and cities of the hills. Jerusalem is a city of stone. The hills sprout and bloom, and the sea becomes stormy and then subsides. But stone is always silent. It doesn't divulge what it was before it became a pile or a wall, or how many years have elapsed since it was first placed there, and what scenes and events it has witnessed in the interim. It zealously keeps everything to itself. It doesn't cast anything out, like the sea, or sprout like the hills.

To live in Jerusalem is to live among stones. Sometimes they provide comfort, other times they provide warmth. But, mostly, they are distant and mysterious. Their presence is so powerful that they do not allow for a routine daily life – rushing off to work, picking up the kids from nursery school, doing the shopping, and feeling relaxed. Routine is fine for other cities but, in Jerusalem, that just isn't possible.

I have lived here for many years and still have a constant sense of missing something. It is as if I am a tourist in a city whose stones are its real residents. They disturb my tranquility, capture my attention, and I pass by them irresponsibly, without stopping to study them, or introduce myself to them so that they'll know and remember that I live here too.

This book is the product of a time-out I took and that I devoted to Jerusalem, or myself, and during which I endeavored to discover the secret of the stones. It is hard to coax stones but even stones can be broken down by prolonged dripping. Slowly but surely I revealed the secrets of some of the stones. The common bond between them is that they are all stones I got to know, and which drew my attention as I rushed about on my everyday business. I wasn't on the lookout for anything new, and I didn't sift through any archeological excavations. Everything was literally right "under my nose," in the most central of places. I took in everything from the corner of my eye and I promised myself I'd return. For example, over the years, when I went to my optician on Yeshayahu Street to order glasses, I'd look out of the window at the old yellow building at the top of the hill. Sometimes the building would be obscured by all the washing hanging out on the balconies, only to re-emerge. As I walked up the hill, I discovered a tiny mosque that, at first glance, looked abandoned. It was only after taking another look that I made out,

every time, the same three people who might have been just slouching around, or cleaning the place. They were always there and they told me about Ukasha, mistakenly taken for a prophet, who was a friend of the prophet Mohammad. Ukasha is buried right here, in the center of the city.

Another time, I hazily realized that archeological excavations had been progressing for some time right under my office window in the Malha Shopping Mall. Every time I looked out, there were the archeologists, piling up sandbags. This went on for several years. When I finally decided to climb the stairs to what looked like a garbage dump in the middle of a parking lot I discovered a whole Byzantine village where, like the mall, there had been a busy commercial life for hundreds of years. I didn't always see everything but I was always alert to stories about stones. Once a Jerusalem photographer told me about an enchanting spot where birthdays could be celebrated in spring. This was a wild park in the Abu Tor neighborhood behind a wall with a gate made of intentionally crooked stone. I remembered the gate and I wanted to know why the stone wasn't straight. When I went there, I saw a gate built like a periscope and I just had to discover the story behind its diagonally hewn stones.

After that it was easier. The stories began to make their way to me under their own steam. There was the one about the lowest sculpture in the world, buried beneath the paving stones in Zion Square, and the well-tended garden in Talpiyyot with two large stones in the center, without anyone knowing what they are. I managed to find a way into the garden and I discovered that this was a monument to Indian soldiers who fought alongside other soldiers of the British Empire in World War I. And there was the rabbi buried beneath a street, and a drapery store with pieces of cloth, all of which contained a thread of gold.

It is hard to say I found everything I wanted. On the contrary, I only touched on the very edges of the story of the stones. I learned a few new things and I got to know some enchanting places. In fact, they were so charming and so anonymous that I felt it would be irresponsible of me to keep them to myself. This book is my way of sharing with as many people as possible a wonderful experience that has had a telling impact on my life.

Tzvia Dobrish-Fried

Who Founded an African Village on the Roof of the Church of the Holy Sepulcher? What Do the Nuns Do at the Sixth Station? Is this a Synagogue or a Church? What Can You Find on the Second Floor of the Drapery Store? What's on Offer at Antioch's Descendants' Museum? Who is Really Buried in the Architects' Grave at Jaffa Gate? Where Can You Find a Neighborhood Oven to Use? What's on the Bridge Over the Way to the Western Wall? How to Get to Vienna Via the Old City? Why is the English Princess Buried in a Russian Church? The House Above the Floor of the Armenian Church. Where Did President Ben-Zvi Find a Quiet Spot? With Whom Did Richard Gere Share the "Fourth Wife's Room"? What Lies Shimmering at the Heart of the Museum? What's Special about Eliyahu's Pita Bread? What is Buddha Doing in a Suburbian House? Who Plays Bowls in the Middle of the Forest? Where Are the Indian Soldiers of His Majesty's Army Buried? What Lurks Near the Entrance to Hell? The Cistern that Became a Hamam, and the Hospital that Became a Hotel. How Much Honor Can the High Commissioner Bestow on the Cat? Who Warmed Themselves by the High Commissioner's Hearth? Is the Gate Crooked or Did the Floor Move? Who Built a White Bench by the Mar Elias Monastery? How Did the Concrete of the Gilo Security Wall become Transparent? Where Did the Animals Go When They Left Noah's Ark? Where Do the Stairs from the Mall Parking Lot Lead? A Work of Art Made to be Walked On. Where is the Brother of the Sundial on Jaffa Road? What Happens at Mahaneh Yehudah Market After the Vegetable Stall Owners Close for the Day? Where is the Entrance to the World's Most Secret Kabbalah Center? Where Did the Greek Patriarch, St. Simon, and Saul Tchernichowski Meet? How Far Were the Limbs of Og, the King of Bashan, Scattered? Where Can You Find Mohammad's Trusty Friend? The Secrets of the Armenian Garden of Eden. After Whom is Jimmy's Alley in the German Colony Named? Who Taught Sir Moses Montefiore to Build the Flour Mill? Who Dared Replace Jerusalem Stone With Tin Plating? The Oldest Villa in Rehavia. Where Are Prayers Translated into Paintings? The Synagogue Over the Catholic Chapel. What Happens When the Rabbi Dies in the Middle of the War? Who Lives Inside the Israel Museum?

The Ethiopian Monks' Village in the Holiest Place in the World!

In the heart of the Old City, on a roof near the Church of the Holy Sepulcher, in the ruins of the Deir es-Sultan monastery, there is an authentic African village. The huts, with the domed roofs, are made of clay, the low doors and windows are painted with gay colors, and all is built around an inner yard with a red crossed-shaped gate.

You access the village by climbing some stairs to the right of the entrance of the Church of the Holy Sepulcher. These lead to the roof of the Church of St. Helen, where the village is located.

A glimpse of the village reveals African men and women in dark robes wearing round velvet hats. These are the Ethiopian monks who live in the village and belong to the Ethiopian Church of Jerusalem.

The huts are dilapidated and shabby looking, and they lean on each other in a huddled group, with barely enough room inside for a single mattress. The Ethiopians, however, insist on living in the village and in the difficult conditions it offers, owing to its proximity to the sacred sites, such as the Via Dolorosa and the Church of the Holy Sepulcher. Growing between the yard and the huts is a thick-trunked tree that is called "the holy olive tree." According to tradition, this is the spot where Abraham brought Isaac to sacrifice him, and it was in the branches of the olive tree that the ram's horns became entangled.

The Christian Ethiopians have been living in Jerusalem for centuries. In the past, they were disposessed of their religious assets in Jerusalem but stubbornly and doggedly regained most of them.

According to Ethiopian tradition, the Ethiopian royal dynasty originates from the liaison between King Solomon and the Queen of Sheba, which produced Emperor Menelik I whom Solomon crowned king of Ethiopia. The traditional belief that Sheba was queen of Ethiopia is also mentioned by Josephus, who calls her Ethiopias in Greek.

The Ethiopian community is first mentioned as living in the city in a bill of rights given by the Caliph Omar Ibn Hattab, who conquered Jerusalem in 636. Later Christian communities made references to the Ethiopians, primarily in letters of Crusaders who visited the city.

The first Ethiopian to be baptized was "the eunuch in charge of the treasures of the Candace [Kandake] Queen of Kush." The emissary Philip met him on his way from Jerusalem to Gaza, and baptized him. According to Ethiopian tradition, this eunuch is called Indak, and he was responsible for persuading Queen Candace to convert to Christianity following which the first Ethiopian church was built in the city of Axum.

Nevertheless, it appears that the Christian approach began in Ethiopia only in the fourth century CE, when two brothers from the city of Tyre, Frumentius and Edusius, persuaded King Azena of Axum to convert to Christianity. Frumentius was appointed by the Patriarch of Alexandria, Athenasius (328–373) as Bishop of Ethiopia in 356. This began the dependency of the Ethiopian church on the Coptic Church, which is known as the church of the early Christians in Egypt. By the end of the fifth century CE, Christianity had been accepted in Ethiopia despite the opposition of some of the aristocracy and the pagan clergy.

Ethiopian monks lived in the Holy Land in the early eras. Their presence in the Holy Land is mentioned several times during the Byzantine Era, particularly in Jerusalem. Archeological excavations have also provided evidence of their being in Jerusalem over the years, in the form of coins and other finds.

The Ethiopian presence in Jerusalem waned during the Ottoman Era, owing to the heavy taxes and detachment from Ethiopia, for political reasons. This led to a decline in the size of the community. This, in turn, resulted in the Ethiopians losing control of most of the holy sites in the seventeenth century, although this did not lead to them leaving the Holy City. Indeed, a short while later they returned and built their village in the church of Deir es-Sultan.

In 1837, the monks living in the village died from a pestilence epidemic but the community returned to life just a few years later. In the last hundred years, the Ethiopian community in the Holy Land has grown. The Ethiopian royal family, and many of the aristocracy there, acquired land and put up buildings for the community's use. Emperor Haile Selassie first visited Jerusalem in 1924, returning in 1933 with his wife Empress Mannan, who bathed in the Jordan River and established a monastery there. In 1936, the couple lived in Jerusalem for several months after fleeing their country following the Italian occupation.

Up to the 1980s, most of the Ethiopian community in Israel consisted of monks who came here for short periods and totaled about 100 people (including 30 nuns). The community was led by an archbishop.

The immigration of Ethiopian Jews to Israel in the 1980s and 1990s also led to the influx of many Christians (who are called, among other terms, Falashmura) who have blood ties with the Jews of Ethiopia, and also include a community of Christians who are not clergymen.

Today, the Ethiopians share the village at Deir es-Sultan with the Copts. It is an uneasy relationship, with power struggles and differences of opinion over control of the site. The Copts have a patriarchate with a church for believers next to the Church of the Holy Sepulcher, parts of which juxtapose the Ethiopian church. But, despite the conflicts, the monks continue to live there with dedication, and zealously hold on to their most sacred site.

The monks live a communal life. They receive pocket money and a separate amount for clothing. The head of the monastery is appointed by the ruler of Ethiopia, and the monks devote most of the day to prayer, particularly between 4 a.m. and 6 a.m., and 4 p.m. and 5 p.m. A festive procession is held there on the Festival of the Cross (Maskal), and another procession with dancing, singing, and playing of instruments is held on the night of the Ethiopian Easter.

On the 27th day of each Ethiopian month (the Ethiopians have their own calendar), a ceremony is held at the monastery marking the tribulations of Jesus, and a ceremony is held marking his birth on the 29th of the month. These festivities have their own special spirit and colors, and they include the use of African artifacts.

Contemporary church customs indicate that the Ethiopians embraced the Bible long before the advent of Christianity. Many of these customs, which originate from the Bible, set the Orthodox Ethiopian church apart from all the other Christian churches. For example, Ethiopian children are circumcised when they are eight days old. They do not eat pork. Saturday and Sunday are rest days, and the elders of the community serve as judges – just like in biblical times. There is a holy ark and a separate area for women in all Ethiopian churches, and the priests dance and sing at religious ceremonies in a manner which, they believe, is reminiscent of the way King David danced before the Ark of the Covenant. Moreover, they do not cross themselves, they adhere to laws of impurity and purification, and the church symbol features a lion, which also symbolizes the tribe of Judah.

The roof of the Church of the Holy Sepulcher, 1 Helena Street, the Old City.

Who Founded an African Village on the Roof of the Church of the Holy Sepulcher? **What Do the Nuns Do at the Sixth Station?** Is this a Synagogue or a Church? What Can You Find on the Second Floor of the Drapery Store? What's on Offer at Antioch's Descendants' Museum? Who is Really Buried in the Architects' Grave at Jaffa Gate? Where Can You Find a Neighborhood Oven to Use? What's on the Bridge Over the Way to the Western Wall? How to Get to Vienna Via the Old City? Why is the English Princess Buried in a Russian Church? The House Above the Floor of the Armenian Church. Where Did President Ben-Zvi Find a Quiet Spot? With Whom Did Richard Gere Share the "Fourth Wife's Room"? What Lies Shimmering at the Heart of the Museum? What's Special about Eliyahu's Pita Bread? What is Buddha Doing in a Suburbian House? Who Plays Bowls in the Middle of the Forest? Where Are the Indian Soldiers of His Majesty's Army Buried? What Lurks Near the Entrance to Hell? The Cistern that Became a Hamam, and the Hospital that Became a Hotel. How Much Honor Can the High Commissioner Bestow on the Cat? Who Warmed Themselves by the High Commissioner's Hearth? Is the Gate Crooked or Did the Floor Move? Who Built a White Bench by the Mar Elias Monastery? How Did the Concrete of the Gilo Security Wall become Transparent? Where Did the Animals Go When They Left Noah's Ark? Where Do the Stairs from the Mall Parking Lot Lead? A Work of Art Made to be Walked On. Where is the Brother of the Sundial on Jaffa Road? What Happens at Mahaneh Yehudah Market After the Vegetable Stall Owners Close for the Day? Where is the Entrance to the World's Most Secret Kabbalah Center? Where Did the Greek Patriarch, St. Simon, and Saul Tchernichowski Meet? How Far Were the Limbs of Og, the King of Bashan, Scattered? Where Can You Find Mohammad's Trusty Friend? The Secrets of the Armenian Garden of Eden. After Whom is Jimmy's Alley in the German Colony Named? Who Taught Sir Moses Montefiore to Build the Flour Mill? Who Dared Replace Jerusalem Stone With Tin Plating? The Oldest Villa in Rehavia. Where Are Prayers Translated into Paintings? The Synagogue Over the Catholic Chapel. What Happens When the Rabbi Dies in the Middle of the War? Who Lives Inside the Israel Museum?

Jesus' Little Sisters Make Paintings

Via Dolorosa is the Way of Sorrow which, according to Christian belief, is the path Jesus took from the court to Mount Golgotha where he was crucified. At the spot called Golgotha, so the story goes, Jesus' blood seeped through a crack in the earth, caused by a tremor, and dripped onto the skull (*"gulgolet"* in Hebrew) of Adam who was buried under the rock, hence the name of the site. The route of the Via Dolorosa starts at Lions' Gate in the Muslim Quarter and ends at the Church of the Holy Sepulcher in the Christian Quarter. The route incorporates 14 stations, of which nine are on the actual route, on Via Dolorosa, and the last five stations inside the Church of the Holy Sepulcher.

Today, following the route of the Via Dolorosa is one the highlights of pilgrims' visits to the Holy Land. However, as Jerusalem was destroyed and rebuilt so many times through the ages, it is hard to reconstruct Jesus' last way. The path taken today along the "way of sorrow" is more a spiritual path of identification with Jesus' suffering and not necessarily an authentic historical route. On occasions pilgrims carry a large heavy wooden cross on their back in order to enhance the religious experience and the sense of identification with their Messiah.

Churches were built at each station, commemorating Jesus' painful experience. All the stations are well known to the pilgrims. It is questionable, however, whether any of the pilgrims have noticed a small niche at the sixth station which houses a workshop, or "atelier," for painting icons. The icons are distributed throughout the world. The artists are none other than genial nuns who belong to the Little Sisters of Jesus monastery, of the Greek Catholic church. All told, the monastery is home to just four nuns who, with their precise paintings, commemorate the suffering of Jesus and what he experienced at the sixth station. This station is the site of the home of Veronica, the woman who came to wipe Jesus' face with a damp cloth. The imprint of Jesus' face was left on the cloth. Traditionally Veronica is identified as the woman dripping in blood depicted in the Gospel of Matthew: "Veronica, a woman who bled for 12 years, approached from behind and touched the edge of his garment, thinking – if I only touch his garment I will be cured. Jesus turned to her and saw her and said: Take courage my daughter. Your faith will save you. From that moment the woman was healed" (Matthew 9:20–22).

Tradition also holds that Veronica was invited to Rome by the Emperor Tiberius who suffered from a serious ailment and was cured by gazing on the cloth. Since the eighth century the cloth has been kept at St. Peter's Church in Rome. The name Veronica probably stems from two words: vera – true, and icon – image.

In 1885 the Greek Catholics built the present church at the sixth station. The church is open to the general public. On the outside the station is marked by a marble pillar embedded in the wall with the name of the place and the number of the station engraved on it. The four painter nuns maintain the church and run a thriving business that allows them to express their artistic bent.

14 Stations along the Via Dolorosa

1. Via Dolorosa starts today at the present day location of the El Omariah School in the Muslim Quarter. This was the site of the Antonia Fortress where, according to Christian tradition, Jesus was tried by the Roman governor Pontius Pilate.
2. The second station is called the Chapel of the Flagellation where, according to Christian tradition, Jesus was whipped by the Roman soldiers after being sentenced to death. Today the site belongs to the Franciscan order and the site contains two churches, an archeological museum, and a bible school.
3. The third station is the place where Jesus fell for the first time. The station was built in 1856 by the Armenian Catholic chapel on the site of the entrance to Al-Sultan Turkish bathhouse.
4. Jesus met his suffering mother at the fourth station. This station is also owned by the Armenian Catholic church which put up a church here in 1881, and which is dedicated to Our Lady of the Spasm.
5. The fifth station is named after Simon of Cyrene who helped Jesus carry the cross. Just who this Simon was is not known, although his name appears to be of Jewish origin.
6. The sixth station is where Veronica wiped Jesus' face.
7. The seventh station is where Jesus fell for the second time under the weight of the cross. It is possible that the tradition resulted from the fact that the station is at the top of a steep ascent. The station is marked by a low chapel from which a stairway leads to a taller chapel. Today, the church is used by the Coptic-Catholic community.

8. At the eighth station Jesus met women of Jerusalem weeping for his fate. The station is close to Golgotha and access to it is blocked.
9. The ninth station symbolizes the spot where Jesus fell for the third time, in what is now the courtyard of the Church of the Holy Sepulcher. It was marked by a stone with a cross. Over time the cross wore away and the station was moved to its present location near the Coptic Church of St. Anthony.
10. The tenth station is the Chapel of the Disrobing of Jesus. The station is at the top of the stairs near to Golgotha and it commemorates the stripping of Jesus described in the Gospel of Matthew: "And they crucified him, and parted his garments, casting lots, and they sat and guarded over him" (Matthew 27:35).
11. The eleventh station is the place where Jesus was nailed to the cross. It is located in the right hand section of Golgotha and belongs to the Franciscans. The altar, which was donated in 1588, is made of silver and was given by Ferdinand I de Medici, Florence. The nailing of Jesus to the cross is described in the Luke: "When they came to the place called Calvary, they crucified him and the criminals there, one on his right, the other on his left. Then Jesus said: 'Father, forgive them, for they know not what they do'" (Luke 23:33–34)
12. Here Jesus died on the cross. The station is located in the left part of Golgotha and is administered by the Greek Orthodox Church. Underneath the altar there is a disc with a socket in the center, marking "the exact spot" of the cross on which Jesus was crucified.
13. This station is marked by an altar that is administered by the Franciscans. It is dedicated to Mary and is called Our Lady of Sorrows. Next to it is a statue of the Madonna brought from Lisbon in 1778. The station commemorates taking Jesus down off the cross. Mary stood here and held Jesus' body in her arms.
14. This station marks Jesus' grave, located inside the Church of the Holy Sepulcher in a place called the Rotunda. This is not universally recognized by all Christians, and some Protestants marked the spot in the Garden Tomb outside the Old City, north of Damascus Gate. Some Christians believe Jesus' resurrection took place, on Sunday, three days after his death. They mark this as the 15th station in order to give the Via Dolorosa an end with a positive significance.

Via Dolorosa, The Old City.

Who Founded an African Village on the Roof of the Church of the Holy Sepulcher? What Do the Nuns Do at the Sixth Station? **Is this a Synagogue or a Church?** What Can You Find on the Second Floor of the Drapery Store? What's on Offer at Antioch's Descendants' Museum? Who is Really Buried in the Architects' Grave at Jaffa Gate? Where Can You Find a Neighborhood Oven to Use? What's on the Bridge Over the Way to the Western Wall? How to Get to Vienna Via the Old City? Why is the English Princess Buried in a Russian Church? The House Above the Floor of the Armenian Church. Where Did President Ben-Zvi Find a Quiet Spot? With Whom Did Richard Gere Share the "Fourth Wife's Room"? What Lies Shimmering at the Heart of the Museum? What's Special about Eliyahu's Pita Bread? What is Buddha Doing in a Suburbian House? Who Plays Bowls in the Middle of the Forest? Where Are the Indian Soldiers of His Majesty's Army Buried? What Lurks Near the Entrance to Hell? The Cistern that Became a Hamam, and the Hospital that Became a Hotel. How Much Honor Can the High Commissioner Bestow on the Cat? Who Warmed Themselves by the High Commissioner's Hearth? Is the Gate Crooked or Did the Floor Move? Who Built a White Bench by the Mar Elias Monastery? How Did the Concrete of the Gilo Security Wall become Transparent? Where Did the Animals Go When They Left Noah's Ark? Where Do the Stairs from the Mall Parking Lot Lead? A Work of Art Made to be Walked On. Where is the Brother of the Sundial on Jaffa Road? What Happens at Mahaneh Yehudah Market After the Vegetable Stall Owners Close for the Day? Where is the Entrance to the World's Most Secret Kabbalah Center? Where Did the Greek Patriarch, St. Simon, and Saul Tchernichowski Meet? How Far Were the Limbs of Og, the King of Bashan, Scattered? Where Can You Find Mohammad's Trusty Friend? The Secrets of the Armenian Garden of Eden. After Whom is Jimmy's Alley in the German Colony Named? Who Taught Sir Moses Montefiore to Build the Flour Mill? Who Dared Replace Jerusalem Stone With Tin Plating? The Oldest Villa in Rehavia. Where Are Prayers Translated into Paintings? The Synagogue Over the Catholic Chapel. What Happens When the Rabbi Dies in the Middle of the War? Who Lives Inside the Israel Museum?

A Church with a Star of David, Instead of a Cross

The initial sense you get when you enter the building opposite the Tower of David in the Old City is that this is a particularly magnificent synagogue. The realization that this is, in fact, a church leaves you completely confused. There are no visible crosses and the building is decorated with verses in Hebrew and Jewish motifs, such as a seven-branch candelabrum, a painting of a Star of David, and the Ten Commandments, which are engraved on the lower part of the eastern wall to look like a Torah ark.

This is, however, indeed a church, Christ Church which was intentionally designed in an ambiguous manner to serve the purposes for which it was built.

Christ Church, which is situated near Jaffa Gate, was the first Protestant church built in the Holy Land, and the whole of the Middle East. It was 1849. The Protestants wanted to convert the Jews, and promote the idea of the millennium – the thousand-year kingdom – which was supposed to start after all the Jews had converted to Christianity, and after the second coming of Jesus.

The church was built by the London Society for the Promotion of Christianity among the Jews, which emerged in the early nineteenth century out of the Protestant movement in England, which initially aimed to restore the people of Israel to their country, culminating with the Jews' acceptance of Jesus.

When the Society's officials arrived in Jerusalem in the 1830s, they looked for a site near the Jewish Quarter to establish their center. The center's missionary work began in earnest with the arrival of the first Protestant bishop in Jerusalem, Bishop Solomon Alexander, a converted Jew who was originally called Michael Solomon Alexander. A descendant of a family of Polish rabbis, he went to Britain at the age of 21 to serve as the rabbi and ritual slaughterer in the communities of Norwich and Plymouth. There he discovered Christianity and was baptized.

The first Protestants saw the difficult living conditions of the Jews in the Jewish Quarter and considered attracting them to

Christianity by offering them assistance and providing them with work and a livelihood. They established a hospital near Christ Church that provided Jews with free medical care. They also set up a school for Jewish children. Vocational training workshops were established in the church compound to teach Jews a trade that would allow them to earn a living.

The church itself was built without any clear indications of Christianity in the hope that this would persuade the Jews who came there for help to come to pray there too. There seem to be no crosses in the church but, in fact, subtly positioned crosses can be found. The church is built in Victorian style, and the floor is cross-shaped. The stained-glass windows have pictures with trees in which, only at second glance, you can see tree trunks in the shape of a cross.

Despite the Jews' physical distress, few turned to the hospital or to the other missionary institutions for help. This was partly due to the fact that the rabbis spoke out against those who applied to the mission for help. The schools quickly became schools for Muslim and Christian children. The Jews steered clear of the hospital built near their quarter. Few attended the workshops in the church courtyard, and nothing succeeded in persuading the Jews to convert.

The Jews were highly suspicious of the assistance the Christians offered them. The efforts of the second British Consul, James Finn, and his wife Elizabeth Anne, to alleviate the Jews' plight also largely failed. The couple set up a farm outside the Old City walls, in the Kerem Avraham neighborhood, a distance away from the missionary institutions. There, Finn employed Jews in productive work. Despite the fact that Finn and his wife did not allow any missionary work to take place on the site, the rabbis viewed his project with hostility.

Armenian Patriarch Street opposite the entrance to the Tower of David Museum, the Old City.

Who Founded an African Village on the Roof of the Church of the Holy Sepulcher? What Do the Nuns Do at the Sixth Station? Is this a Synagogue or a Church? **What Can You Find on the Second Floor of the Drapery Store?** What's on Offer at Antioch's Descendants' Museum? Who is Really Buried in the Architects' Grave at Jaffa Gate? Where Can You Find a Neighborhood Oven to Use? What's on the Bridge Over the Way to the Western Wall? How to Get to Vienna Via the Old City? Why is the English Princess Buried in a Russian Church? The House Above the Floor of the Armenian Church. Where Did President Ben-Zvi Find a Quiet Spot? With Whom Did Richard Gere Share the "Fourth Wife's Room"? What Lies Shimmering at the Heart of the Museum? What's Special about Eliyahu's Pita Bread? What is Buddha Doing in a Suburbian House? Who Plays Bowls in the Middle of the Forest? Where Are the Indian Soldiers of His Majesty's Army Buried? What Lurks Near the Entrance to Hell? The Cistern that Became a Hamam, and the Hospital that Became a Hotel. How Much Honor Can the High Commissioner Bestow on the Cat? Who Warmed Themselves by the High Commissioner's Hearth? Is the Gate Crooked or Did the Floor Move? Who Built a White Bench by the Mar Elias Monastery? How Did the Concrete of the Gilo Security Wall become Transparent? Where Did the Animals Go When They Left Noah's Ark? Where Do the Stairs from the Mall Parking Lot Lead? A Work of Art Made to be Walked On. Where is the Brother of the Sundial on Jaffa Road? What Happens at Mahaneh Yehudah Market After the Vegetable Stall Owners Close for the Day? Where is the Entrance to the World's Most Secret Kabbalah Center? Where Did the Greek Patriarch, St. Simon, and Saul Tchernichowski Meet? How Far Were the Limbs of Og, the King of Bashan, Scattered? Where Can You Find Mohammad's Trusty Friend? The Secrets of the Armenian Garden of Eden. After Whom is Jimmy's Alley in the German Colony Named? Who Taught Sir Moses Montefiore to Build the Flour Mill? Who Dared Replace Jerusalem Stone With Tin Plating? The Oldest Villa in Rehavia. Where Are Prayers Translated into Paintings? The Synagogue Over the Catholic Chapel. What Happens When the Rabbi Dies in the Middle of the War? Who Lives Inside the Israel Museum?

Stories Entwined in Golden Thread

To the casual visitor, Ibrahim Abu Khallaf's establishment looks just like any other textile store. The long, high shelves along the walls are stacked with fabrics, rolls of dark cloth for men's suits, and piles of airy, colorful cloth for women's dresses. The place is a model of tidiness.

At the end of the narrow store, in the dark part next to the counter, two nuns are taking advice from the store owner. A Canadian tourist who specifically came to the store waits patiently at one side. A Hasid in a striped garment enters and hurriedly leaves, promising to return when the women leave the store. What is so special about this store that such a diverse clientele go there, to 98 ha-Notzerim Street (Christians Street), in the Old City market? What are they all looking for?

The mystery becomes clear when you climb to the second floor. When you ascend the narrow stairs which, too, are laden with fabrics, you suddenly find an incredible wealth of colors – red, pink, bright blue and, primarily, shining gold. Oriental fabrics hang down on all sides, and the desks are weighed down with fabrics that have been heaped up on them.

While the tidy first floor gets scant attention – in the age of industrialized production, few actually sew dresses and suits themselves – the enchanting colorful fabrics on the second floor, which look like something out of *Arabian Nights*, are in great demand.

The fabrics are carefully selected and come from just four countries: Syria, Egypt, Morocco, and India. They are bought not only for their aesthetic qualities but also for reasons of tradition and quality. They have to be made of natural materials and hand woven. Many have time-tested patterns, fixed colors, and an ancient tale to tell. Others are so thick they could be used to upholster furniture, even though they are meant to be used for garments. Few know, for example, that the stripes on the Syrian fabrics symbolize the flowing water of the rivers. For generations and generations, these fabrics have been used the world over to make expensive sheets and table cloths while in this part of the world, they are used to make the striped garments of Hasidim from the court of Rabbi Aaron.

In Damascus, a special brocade is made called the "museum brocade," which has the set image of a peacock with a colorful tail, of Crusaders leaving for battle, or of Saladin. This fabric is mainly used for luxurious clothes for priests and bishops to wear at festive ceremonies.

The brocade and heavy and rich tapestry cloth come from India. They are of such high quality that, although they were originally designed to make saris for wealthy women, they can also be used for upholstering and for curtains. The cotton, considered to be the best in the world, comes from Egypt. It is so fine that it feels like expensive silk.

However, the crowning jewel in the store is undoubtedly a fabric called *"melekh"* (king), which is a plain fabric with two colored stripes. In the past, the fabric was used to make expensive brides' dresses, and today it is used to decorate church altars or as furniture upholstery.

Ibrahim's store has operated from the same place for generations, but it is only recently that the public has begun to appreciate the hand-woven fabrics, made of natural materials, whose beauty modern techniques could never replicate. Who would have believed that the colorful furniture in expensive homes or the heavy curtains that look almost unaffordable are, in fact, made of fabrics that Ibrahim sells on the second floor of his store on ha-Notzerim Street in the Old City?

98 ha-Notsrim (Christians) Street, The Old City market.

Who Founded an African Village on the Roof of the Church of the Holy Sepulcher? What Do the Nuns Do at the Sixth Station? Is this a Synagogue or a Church? What Can You Find on the Second Floor of the Drapery Store? **What's on Offer at Antioch's Descendants' Museum?** Who is Really Buried in the Architects' Grave at Jaffa Gate? Where Can You Find a Neighborhood Oven to Use? What's on the Bridge Over the Way to the Western Wall? How to Get to Vienna Via the Old City? Why is the English Princess Buried in a Russian Church? The House Above the Floor of the Armenian Church. Where Did President Ben-Zvi Find a Quiet Spot? With Whom Did Richard Gere Share the "Fourth Wife's Room"? What Lies Shimmering at the Heart of the Museum? What's Special about Eliyahu's Pita Bread? What is Buddha Doing in a Suburbian House? Who Plays Bowls in the Middle of the Forest? Where Are the Indian Soldiers of His Majesty's Army Buried? What Lurks Near the Entrance to Hell? The Cistern that Became a Hamam, and the Hospital that Became a Hotel. How Much Honor Can the High Commissioner Bestow on the Cat? Who Warmed Themselves by the High Commissioner's Hearth? Is the Gate Crooked or Did the Floor Move? Who Built a White Bench by the Mar Elias Monastery? How Did the Concrete of the Gilo Security Wall become Transparent? Where Did the Animals Go When They Left Noah's Ark? Where Do the Stairs from the Mall Parking Lot Lead? A Work of Art Made to be Walked On. Where is the Brother of the Sundial on Jaffa Road? What Happens at Mahaneh Yehudah Market After the Vegetable Stall Owners Close for the Day? Where is the Entrance to the World's Most Secret Kabbalah Center? Where Did the Greek Patriarch, St. Simon, and Saul Tchernichowski Meet? How Far Were the Limbs of Og, the King of Bashan, Scattered? Where Can You Find Mohammad's Trusty Friend? The Secrets of the Armenian Garden of Eden. After Whom is Jimmy's Alley in the German Colony Named? Who Taught Sir Moses Montefiore to Build the Flour Mill? Who Dared Replace Jerusalem Stone With Tin Plating? The Oldest Villa in Rehavia. Where Are Prayers Translated into Paintings? The Synagogue Over the Catholic Chapel. What Happens When the Rabbi Dies in the Middle of the War? Who Lives Inside the Israel Museum?

The Fashion of Jerusalem Monks through the Ages

To the left of Jaffa Gate, and up to David Street, the street where the Old City market starts, lies a web of narrow alleyways, all of which lead to the Christian Quarter.

This is a peaceful and remarkably clean quarter, although it comes alive in the evenings. Families take a stroll with their children, neighbors chat across balcony railings and old ladies, wending their way home from the stores laden with baskets, stop to chat to one of the many priests who live there. As the alleys are so narrow, very few vehicles pass by to disturb the youths playing with a ball in the middle of the street.

The human backdrop here is different from the other quarters of the Old City. There is no sign of the long dresses of the women of the Jewish Quarter, nor of the veils of the Muslim Quarter. The young girls wear school uniforms with short dresses, and the boys wear fashionable jeans. The priests with their dark costumes, who fill the quarter, do nothing to offset the liberal atmosphere. Nor do the dozens of churches hidden between the houses. One must remember that most of the Christian orders have a church, patriarchate, or representation in this quarter.

One of the largest orders is the Greek Catholic order. The church has its roots in the Roman Empire, and that is why they include the word "Melkite" (coming from the Syriac word for imperial) in their name – the Melkite Greek Catholic Church. This was the official patriarchy of Antioch, the kingdom of Antiochus, who ruled in this region after the death of Alexander the Great. The church has 1,700,000 followers around the world, half a million of whom live in the Middle East.

The Greek Catholics have several institutions in the Christian Quarter, and they are hidden between houses and behind modest looking doorways. The patriarchate is located on Greek Patriarchate Street, and it incorporates the splendid center of the Catholic Greeks in Jerusalem. The patriarchate was established in Jerusalem in 1341. The church and the center from which it operates were built in 1848. The center also houses a small hotel for pilgrims and an unusual museum.

This is a small and simple looking museum containing authentic documentation of the fashions worn by monks in Jerusalem. The person who initiated the museum is the present patriarch of the Greek Catholic church in Jerusalem, Antioch, and Alexandria, Gregory III Lakam, who previously served as archbishop of the church in Jerusalem.

The museum, which is nurtured and maintained by monks, serves as a tribute to all the Eastern Churches in Israel and is called The Museum of the Eastern Churches. The museum houses an impressive collection of garments worn by monks and nuns, and it presents examples and explains the dress customs of each church and order as well as of the various sects in Israel, and the differences between them: what crucifixes they use, which prayer beads, and the reasons for the differences.

The museum contains figures of Syrian Christian priests who spoke Aramaic and originated from Antioch in Syria; Coptic priests from Alexandria, Egypt, who wore cloaks and tight embroidered caps; dark skinned Ethiopian monks wearing white robes; Russian monks and nuns; Greek Orthodox monks; Armenian monks with their unique pointed black head coverings; Maronite monks, of whom there are only a few in Israel, with most living in Lebanon; and an Assyrian monk.

The museum contains a collection of various sacred artifacts from different orders, such as crucifixes, a semandron, a small wooden bell used to call monks to prayer seven times a day; a rafidia, a figure with angel wings; antimensium, cloths used to cover altars; and prayer beads, some with 33 beads, some with 100, and others with 300. The beads are meant to help the worshipper concentrate and repeat the same words over and over. "Jesus the Messiah, the son of God, have mercy on me, the sinner." The number of beads and the repetition of the same words are meant to assist the worshipper to achieve a high level of concentration, until it becomes part of the prayer itself.

The museum also contains a collection of icons, Easter eggs, and a typical altar which, it is explained, symbolizes Jesus and his grave. The rich covering over the altar symbolizes Jesus' shroud. The wine cup on the altar symbolizes the blood of Jesus, and the bread – his flesh. There is a copper bird hanging above the altar, with sacramental bread to be given to the poor placed in its sunken center.

The Greek Catholics wish to use the museum to demonstrate their respect for all the other Christians in Israel, but also to expose their followers to other beliefs and other Christian sects, and to work to achieve harmony among them. A brief visit to the small museum, as well as a visit to the delightful church next to it, provides an intriguing and surprising experience which explains all facets relating to Christian life in Jerusalem.

Greek Patriarchate Street, the Christian Quarter, the Old City.

Who Founded an African Village on the Roof of the Church of the Holy Sepulcher? What Do the Nuns Do at the Sixth Station? Is this a Synagogue or a Church? What Can You Find on the Second Floor of the Drapery Store? What's on Offer at Antioch's Descendants' Museum? **Who is Really Buried in the Architects' Grave at Jaffa Gate?** Where Can You Find a Neighborhood Oven to Use? What's on the Bridge Over the Way to the Western Wall? How to Get to Vienna Via the Old City? Why is the English Princess Buried in a Russian Church? The House Above the Floor of the Armenian Church. Where Did President Ben-Zvi Find a Quiet Spot? With Whom Did Richard Gere Share the "Fourth Wife's Room"? What Lies Shimmering at the Heart of the Museum? What's Special about Eliyahu's Pita Bread? What is Buddha Doing in a Suburbian House? Who Plays Bowls in the Middle of the Forest? Where Are the Indian Soldiers of His Majesty's Army Buried? What Lurks Near the Entrance to Hell? The Cistern that Became a Hamam, and the Hospital that Became a Hotel. How Much Honor Can the High Commissioner Bestow on the Cat? Who Warmed Themselves by the High Commissioner's Hearth? Is the Gate Crooked or Did the Floor Move? Who Built a White Bench by the Mar Elias Monastery? How Did the Concrete of the Gilo Security Wall become Transparent? Where Did the Animals Go When They Left Noah's Ark? Where Do the Stairs from the Mall Parking Lot Lead? A Work of Art Made to be Walked On. Where is the Brother of the Sundial on Jaffa Road? What Happens at Mahaneh Yehudah Market After the Vegetable Stall Owners Close for the Day? Where is the Entrance to the World's Most Secret Kabbalah Center? Where Did the Greek Patriarch, St. Simon, and Saul Tchernichowski Meet? How Far Were the Limbs of Og, the King of Bashan, Scattered? Where Can You Find Mohammad's Trusty Friend? The Secrets of the Armenian Garden of Eden. After Whom is Jimmy's Alley in the German Colony Named? Who Taught Sir Moses Montefiore to Build the Flour Mill? Who Dared Replace Jerusalem Stone With Tin Plating? The Oldest Villa in Rehavia. Where Are Prayers Translated into Paintings? The Synagogue Over the Catholic Chapel. What Happens When the Rabbi Dies in the Middle of the War? Who Lives Inside the Israel Museum?

The Truth Has Three Versions

There is a thin line, in Jerusalem, between stories and legends, and historical facts. There are stories that have been around in the city for hundreds of years that, over time, have turned into facts. Historical reality is no longer of consequence. The ancient legend has almost replaced it.

The case of the Turkish architects' grave at Jaffa Gate is a prime example of this. The burial plot is on a raised platform on the north side of the entrance area of the gate, behind a heavy iron fence, and a wide tree, which protect the graves. These are actually two graves with impressive tombstones, having a sculpted turban on each.

One of the stories about these graves, which has been passed down the generations, is that they are the graves of the two architects who planned and built the wall surrounding the Old City at the behest of the Turkish sultan Suleiman the Magnificent.

When they completed the construction, Suleiman ordered them to be executed by hanging. The all-powerful ruler decided to kill them to ensure the secret of the construction work would never be revealed. Suleiman had ordered secret openings and hiding places to be built into the wall and, besides the architects, only Suleiman knew about them.

Another story relates that Suleiman the Magnificent wanted to make sure that no other place in the world would have such a magnificent wall. With the death of the architects, he remained alone with his wall and its secrets.

There is also an ancient legend about the architects' grave that says that the architects were beheaded when Suleiman discovered that, despite his explicit order, they had decided not enclose Mount Zion inside the wall. This significantly shortened the wall and thus allowed the architects to pocket a large sum of money, which was the difference between their fee and the actual cost of construction.

When Suleiman discovered the deceit he ordered the architects to be beheaded and for them to be buried in an opening in the wall they, themselves, had built. This was done to make an example of the architects, to convey to Suleiman's subjects that no one should try to cheat him.

Surprisingly, despite its geographical position, Mount Zion is not included in the Old City walls. The present wall was built in 1540 on the ruins of earlier ancient walls – the wall from the time of the Second Temple, the wall from the Roman Era, one from the Byzantine period, and one from the Middle Ages. Suleiman the Magnificent's wall starts from the Tower of David. After Jaffa Gate, it turns northward and encompasses the Christian Quarter. It then continues on to the New Gate, from which it runs down to Damascus Gate. From there it drops down, over rocks, to Herod's Gate, which is also known as the Flowers Gate. Thereafter, the wall continues in an easterly direction until the corner known as "Bourj Laqlaq" – the stork's fortress – and from there to the south, to the Muslim cemetery, and thereafter to the Lions' Gate.

This gate has a pair of lions – the symbol of the Turkish rule – carved into it. A short distance from the gate, the wall runs around the Temple courtyard. There is a blocked gate, the Golden Gate, at the edge of Mount Moriah.

From there the wall continues to the south to the Dung Gate, climbs up steeply to Mount Zion, and passes along the edge of the Jewish Quarter to Zion Gate. The wall then leaves out Mount Zion, and continues westwards to complete the circuit at the Tower of David.

Between 1948 and 1967, part of the wall that circumnavigates Mount Zion served as the front line between Israel and Jordan. Mount Zion, which remained in Israeli control, attracted many Jews who came to look out over the Old City and at the holy places they could not reach at the time.

Why did Suleiman decide to build a wall in Jerusalem after it had lain in ruins during the Mameluk Period? The reason is unclear. It may have been an act of bravado, to demonstrate the importance of the city to the Turks, the new conquerors. The wall also acted as a buffer, to keep out nomads, who may have endangered the

security of the inhabitants, or it may have been built because of the Ottomans' concern that there might be another crusade by the Catholic countries of Europe. Whatever the real reason, Jerusalem got its famous wall, a significant structure and central element of the city's visual and spiritual image.

To date, no historical evidence has been unearthed to authenticate the stories about the two architects. Moreover, there are similar stories about the architects who built the Taj Mahal in India, that relate that the designers were buried within the wall that surrounds the magnificent temple to prevent the secret of the construction from being revealed. The questions about the two graves at the entrance of the Old City arose because, in those days, the dead were buried outside the city walls, and here are two impressive graves right inside the wall, and in a place of honor near Jaffa Gate. The location of the graves contradicted accepted practice at the time. The reasons for this were not clear, and this gave rise to the stories about the two honorable and mysterious dead people. The degree of historical truth behind the myth of the architects is not known but, no doubt, it lies waiting to be found.

The Jaffa Gate plaza. The Old City.

Who Founded an African Village on the Roof of the Church of the Holy Sepulcher? What Do the Nuns Do at the Sixth Station? Is this a Synagogue or a Church? What Can You Find on the Second Floor of the Drapery Store? What's on Offer at Antioch's Descendants' Museum? Who is Really Buried in the Architects' Grave at Jaffa Gate? **Where Can You Find a Neighborhood Oven to Use?** What's on the Bridge Over the Way to the Western Wall? How to Get to Vienna Via the Old City? Why is the English Princess Buried in a Russian Church? The House Above the Floor of the Armenian Church. Where Did President Ben-Zvi Find a Quiet Spot? With Whom Did Richard Gere Share the "Fourth Wife's Room"? What Lies Shimmering at the Heart of the Museum? What's Special about Eliyahu's Pita Bread? What is Buddha Doing in a Suburbian House? Who Plays Bowls in the Middle of the Forest? Where Are the Indian Soldiers of His Majesty's Army Buried? What Lurks Near the Entrance to Hell? The Cistern that Became a Hamam, and the Hospital that Became a Hotel. How Much Honor Can the High Commissioner Bestow on the Cat? Who Warmed Themselves by the High Commissioner's Hearth? Is the Gate Crooked or Did the Floor Move? Who Built a White Bench by the Mar Elias Monastery? How Did the Concrete of the Gilo Security Wall become Transparent? Where Did the Animals Go When They Left Noah's Ark? Where Do the Stairs from the Mall Parking Lot Lead? A Work of Art Made to be Walked On. Where is the Brother of the Sundial on Jaffa Road? What Happens at Mahaneh Yehudah Market After the Vegetable Stall Owners Close for the Day? Where is the Entrance to the World's Most Secret Kabbalah Center? Where Did the Greek Patriarch, St. Simon, and Saul Tchernichowski Meet? How Far Were the Limbs of Og, the King of Bashan, Scattered? Where Can You Find Mohammad's Trusty Friend? The Secrets of the Armenian Garden of Eden. After Whom is Jimmy's Alley in the German Colony Named? Who Taught Sir Moses Montefiore to Build the Flour Mill? Who Dared Replace Jerusalem Stone With Tin Plating? The Oldest Villa in Rehavia. Where Are Prayers Translated into Paintings? The Synagogue Over the Catholic Chapel. What Happens When the Rabbi Dies in the Middle of the War? Who Lives Inside the Israel Museum?

Running around the Alleyways with Pots

There are several ways to identify a genuine Jerusalemite. He'll always pay a visit to Mazmil House but doesn't go to the Kiryat ha-Yovel neighborhood. He builds a house with beautiful stonework but puts an ugly water container on the roof just in case there's another siege on Jerusalem, and he always waxes on nostalgically about stories of the Jerusalem oven.

The stories of the Jerusalem oven have become the stuff of legend, and they have long since exceeded the city's boundaries via the communications lines of the play *Bustan Sephardi* and the broadband technology of the Gashash Hiver comedy team. In Haifa, for example, where they know the story well, they can't adapt the tale to a Haifa oven simply because this is a typical Jerusalem story.

Many years ago, as legend has it, on Fridays in the days when homes did not have baking ovens, each family would prepare a pot of *hamin* (slow-cooking stew) for the Sabbath. They would tie an identifying thread around the pot and send the youngest son off with it to the nearby bakery. The bakery, which worked the oven (or *taboun*) 24 hours a day during the week, turned the oven off before the Sabbath. However, as the oven was the only one for miles around, and it retained its heat long after being turned off, all the locals would bring their pot of *hamin*, with brightly colored thread attached to it to differentiate it from the others, and place it in the oven, leaving it there overnight. The following day, the child would return to the bakery and pick up the pot. The *hamin*, as the story goes, had a special flavor which simply cannot be replicated today. There are also stories of "mix-ups," with others' pots being taken "by mistake." Everyone knew who the best cooks in the neighborhood were, and whose pot was worth taking "by mistake."

Today, it is easier to find remains of the Temple in Jerusalem than a neighborhood oven. A *talmud torah* (religious elementary school) was built over the neighborhood oven in the Bukharan Quarter many years ago, and no one knew how to tell me to find Abadi's oven in the Beit Yaakov neighborhood. I'd grown up, however, with the legend and the story of the unique flavor of the *hamin* that had cooked through the night in the glowing embers, and I just

had to try and find the lost oven. In the end, after much effort and long searching, I found that the oven has survived to this day.

The large oven, made of red clay and covered with tiles that were once white, was found at the Se'or bakery at 54 ha-Notzerim (Christians) Street in the Old City market. It provides evidence that it wasn't only the Jews who suffered poverty and couldn't afford their own ovens, and that the Arabs suffered the same fate. The custom of running through the alleyways, and eventually placing the pot on the family table, transcends walls, wars, and nationalities. This proved that the story of the oven was real, and not just the stuff of legend.

Today, the oven at the Se'or bakery is used to make pita bread. At night, large beautiful pottery or copper pots with vegetables, meat and rice are placed in it to cook. These are, however, not the pots of the neighbors brought from their homes. They are the pots of the owner who uses them to prepare delicacies. The city's residents order dishes from the bakery owner and he prepares them according to the old method, like an old trusty catering service. Today, you can still take a nostalgic trip back through time and taste a bit of Jerusalem history.

54 ha-Notsrim (Christians) Street, the Old City market.

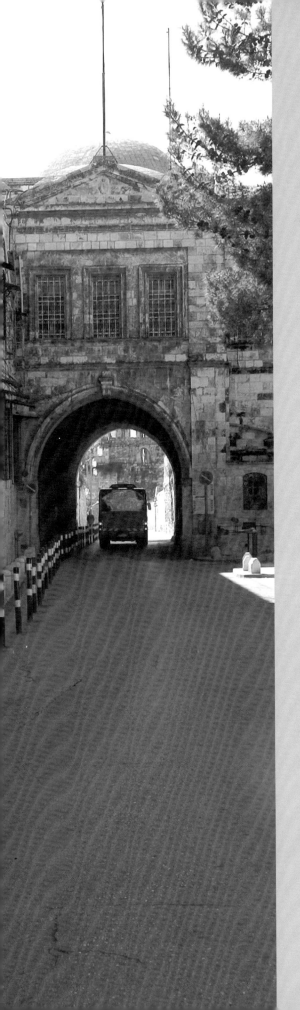

Who Founded an African Village on the Roof of the Church of the Holy Sepulcher? What Do the Nuns Do at the Sixth Station? Is this a Synagogue or a Church? What Can You Find on the Second Floor of the Drapery Store? What's on Offer at Antioch's Descendants' Museum? Who is Really Buried in the Architects' Grave at Jaffa Gate? Where Can You Find a Neighborhood Oven to Use? **What's on the Bridge Over the Way to the Western Wall?** How to Get to Vienna Via the Old City? Why is the English Princess Buried in a Russian Church? The House Above the Floor of the Armenian Church. Where Did President Ben-Zvi Find a Quiet Spot? With Whom Did Richard Gere Share the "Fourth Wife's Room"? What Lies Shimmering at the Heart of the Museum? What's Special about Eliyahu's Pita Bread? What is Buddha Doing in a Suburbian House? Who Plays Bowls in the Middle of the Forest? Where Are the Indian Soldiers of His Majesty's Army Buried? What Lurks Near the Entrance to Hell? The Cistern that Became a Hamam, and the Hospital that Became a Hotel. How Much Honor Can the High Commissioner Bestow on the Cat? Who Warmed Themselves by the High Commissioner's Hearth? Is the Gate Crooked or Did the Floor Move? Who Built a White Bench by the Mar Elias Monastery? How Did the Concrete of the Gilo Security Wall become Transparent? Where Did the Animals Go When They Left Noah's Ark? Where Do the Stairs from the Mall Parking Lot Lead? A Work of Art Made to be Walked On. Where is the Brother of the Sundial on Jaffa Road? What Happens at Mahaneh Yehudah Market After the Vegetable Stall Owners Close for the Day? Where is the Entrance to the World's Most Secret Kabbalah Center? Where Did the Greek Patriarch, St. Simon, and Saul Tchernichowski Meet? How Far Were the Limbs of Og, the King of Bashan, Scattered? Where Can You Find Mohammad's Trusty Friend? The Secrets of the Armenian Garden of Eden. After Whom is Jimmy's Alley in the German Colony Named? Who Taught Sir Moses Montefiore to Build the Flour Mill? Who Dared Replace Jerusalem Stone With Tin Plating? The Oldest Villa in Rehavia. Where Are Prayers Translated into Paintings? The Synagogue Over the Catholic Chapel. What Happens When the Rabbi Dies in the Middle of the War? Who Lives Inside the Israel Museum?

The Whole Palace Is One Narrow Bridge

Every old city in the world has narrow streets and cramped alleys that, in the interest of progress, were turned into roads wide enough for cars to use.

In the Old City of Jerusalem, on the way to the Western Wall, there are alleys which were once suitable only for mules, or for horses with carts, but found it hard to accommodate cars. Once in a while, particularly wide vehicles lose a wing mirror or a strip or two of paint en route. The cars "repay" the alleyways by leaving a coat of soot on the walls of adjoining houses and even scrape off some of the plaster from the walls. But, damage and minor accidents notwithstanding, daring drivers who want to get to the Western Wall via the Armenian Quarter can enjoy some intriguing experiences.

The Armenian Quarter is one of the most beautiful of all the neighborhoods, stretching from Jaffa Gate as far as the Jewish Quarter. It lies opposite the Kishla building that once served as an Ottoman prison and is now used as the Old City police station.

The Armenian Quarter includes the Armenian church, which acts as the hub of daily life in the quarter, and residential buildings belonging to the church which are rented out to Armenians at particularly low rates. The compound is enclosed by a wall, and its gates are locked every evening at ten o'clock. Latecomers have to pre-arrange to have the gate opened on their return.

The wide street ends at Jaffa Gate and turns into a bustling market square full of vendors with one-wheeled carts, which are probably the most suitable vehicle for the market streets. You can't drive on straight ahead because the alley is too narrow and is stepped. You have to turn right, although this part of the road is also narrow and winds its way between tightly packed houses that don't seem to leave enough room for cars to pass. Armenian Patriarchate Street is the drivers' path of suffering – their Via Dolorosa – as they slowly squirm their way along the road, taking care not to hit any walls that could pop out to surprise them at any moment.

Drivers would do well not to take their eyes off the narrow road. Even so, it is worth their knowing that, right at the start of the narrow road to the Western Wall, there is a handsome, ornate, rounded bridge with arched windows barred by stylized grilles, with a brightly lit interior.

The bridge wasn't put there to provide shelter from the rain, and not for pedestrians. In fact, the bridge contains a beautiful sitting room in a private house. The room is furnished with antique furniture, large crystal chandeliers, and heavy English carpets, and there is an atmosphere of sumptuousness that can only be partially glimpsed from the outside. The other rooms of the house are on the left side of the bridge, and there is a flower garden with large marble sculptures to the right.

This is the home of the Armenian patriarch on the edge of the Armenian Quarter. The house was built inside the bridge in 1853. This was because Ottoman law at the time prohibited the construction of more houses at ground level in the Old City, due to the shortage of space. In order to bypass the legal restriction, and to help alleviate the shortage of housing for Armenians at the time, the bridge was built over the alleyway in a single night, and a house was built on top of it. This provided a housing solution in the air.

The bridge, which, from the outside looks small and narrow, has, in fact, a spacious interior. It is wide and very high. The windows that are visible from the street are located high up on the walls and a ladder is needed to open and close them. The house also contains workrooms and large impressive reception rooms as well as a small bedroom and a tiny dining room designed for a single person. This is because the Armenian patriarch is prohibited from marrying and having children. Today, the house is inhabited by the 96th Armenian patriarch, Torkom Manoogian.

The patriarch's home is known to few, both because entrance to it is prohibited and due to its extraordinary position. It is possibly, because of this that we all pass by beneath it without looking up to marvel at it.

The Patriarch's Bridge, Armenian Patriarchate Street, the Old City.

Who Founded an African Village on the Roof of the Church of the Holy Sepulcher? What Do the Nuns Do at the Sixth Station? Is this a Synagogue or a Church? What Can You Find on the Second Floor of the Drapery Store? What's on Offer at Antioch's Descendants' Museum? Who is Really Buried in the Architects' Grave at Jaffa Gate? Where Can You Find a Neighborhood Oven to Use? What's on the Bridge Over the Way to the Western Wall? How to Get to Vienna Via the Old City? Why is the English Princess Buried in a Russian Church? The House Above the Floor of the Armenian Church. Where Did President Ben-Zvi Find a Quiet Spot? With Whom Did Richard Gere Share the "Fourth Wife's Room"? What Lies Shimmering at the Heart of the Museum? What's Special about Eliyahu's Pita Bread? What is Buddha Doing in a Suburbian House? Who Plays Bowls in the Middle of the Forest? Where Are the Indian Soldiers of His Majesty's Army Buried? What Lurks Near the Entrance to Hell? The Cistern that Became a Hamam, and the Hospital that Became a Hotel. How Much Honor Can the High Commissioner Bestow on the Cat? Who Warmed Themselves by the High Commissioner's Hearth? Is the Gate Crooked or Did the Floor Move? Who Built a White Bench by the Mar Elias Monastery? How Did the Concrete of the Gilo Security Wall become Transparent? Where Did the Animals Go When They Left Noah's Ark? Where Do the Stairs from the Mall Parking Lot Lead? A Work of Art Made to be Walked On. Where is the Brother of the Sundial on Jaffa Road? What Happens at Mahaneh Yehudah Market After the Vegetable Stall Owners Close for the Day? Where is the Entrance to the World's Most Secret Kabbalah Center? Where Did the Greek Patriarch, St. Simon, and Saul Tchernichowski Meet? How Far Were the Limbs of Og, the King of Bashan, Scattered? Where Can You Find Mohammad's Trusty Friend? The Secrets of the Armenian Garden of Eden. After Whom is Jimmy's Alley in the German Colony Named? Who Taught Sir Moses Montefiore to Build the Flour Mill? Who Dared Replace Jerusalem Stone With Tin Plating? The Oldest Villa in Rehavia. Where Are Prayers Translated into Paintings? The Synagogue Over the Catholic Chapel. What Happens When the Rabbi Dies in the Middle of the War? Who Lives Inside the Israel Museum?

Strudel in the Muslim Quarter Market

On the plate in front of me is a slice of flaky strudel, with a generous spoonful of sweet whipped cream next to it. The portion is, of course, served with a cup of hot strong coffee but the strudel is long gone before the coffee turns cold.

During the summer months, the delicacy is served on the shaded balcony or in the raised garden that overlooks the busy street below. On rainy days, the food is served next to the black grand piano, in the elegant drawing room, with the ceiling decorated in bright colors and frescoes.

The menu is beautifully designed, and the food is served immaculately. There is a quiet European ambiance inside, despite the fact that this is not exactly an inn somewhere in the Tyrol region of Austria, but an Austrian hospice on the Via Dolorosa, not far from the Damascus Gate in the Muslim Quarter of the Old City.

The hustle and bustle of the street do not carry over the high walls of the hospice. The women, covered from head to toe, shopping in the market, don't enter the iron gate, and none of the guests at the hospice seem to belong in the busy street below. Here all is polite quietness and courteousness.

The hospice, which now serves as a hotel, and the garden attract all strudel lovers to them. The hospice was built in 1863 as a hostel for Austrian pilgrims who were interested in visiting Jerusalem. Later a hospital was established there, which was first used to treat Austrian pilgrims and later Arabs from the Old City.

In 1869, the Austrian Emperor Franz Joseph, whose many titles included "King of Jerusalem," stayed at the hospice. After his visit, the hospice became a hotel used by members of the Austrian aristocracy who followed the emperor to Jerusalem.

During the British Mandate, the hospice closed, and the building was used as a college for British officers. It wasn't until 1985 that the property was returned by the Israeli government to its owners, the Austrian government. This was facilitated by then mayor of Jerusalem, Teddy Kollek, who was born in Austria and was a supporter of the hospice. Since then, the hospice has operated as a hotel for anyone looking for some European ambiance, and an island of sanity in the middle of the daily hubbub of Jerusalem.

7 Via Dolorosa, the Muslim Quarter, the Old City.

Who Founded an African Village on the Roof of the Church of the Holy Sepulcher? What Do the Nuns Do at the Sixth Station? Is this a Synagogue or a Church? What Can You Find on the Second Floor of the Drapery Store? What's on Offer at Antioch's Descendants' Museum? Who is Really Buried in the Architects' Grave at Jaffa Gate? Where Can You Find a Neighborhood Oven to Use? What's on the Bridge Over the Way to the Western Wall? How to Get to Vienna Via the Old City? **Why is the English Princess Buried in a Russian Church?** The House Above the Floor of the Armenian Church. Where Did President Ben-Zvi Find a Quiet Spot? With Whom Did Richard Gere Share the "Fourth Wife's Room"? What Lies Shimmering at the Heart of the Museum? What's Special about Eliyahu's Pita Bread? What is Buddha Doing in a Suburbian House? Who Plays Bowls in the Middle of the Forest? Where Are the Indian Soldiers of His Majesty's Army Buried? What Lurks Near the Entrance to Hell? The Cistern that Became a Hamam, and the Hospital that Became a Hotel. How Much Honor Can the High Commissioner Bestow on the Cat? Who Warmed Themselves by the High Commissioner's Hearth? Is the Gate Crooked or Did the Floor Move? Who Built a White Bench by the Mar Elias Monastery? How Did the Concrete of the Gilo Security Wall become Transparent? Where Did the Animals Go When They Left Noah's Ark? Where Do the Stairs from the Mall Parking Lot Lead? A Work of Art Made to be Walked On. Where is the Brother of the Sundial on Jaffa Road? What Happens at Mahaneh Yehudah Market After the Vegetable Stall Owners Close for the Day? Where is the Entrance to the World's Most Secret Kabbalah Center? Where Did the Greek Patriarch, St. Simon, and Saul Tchernichowski Meet? How Far Were the Limbs of Og, the King of Bashan, Scattered? Where Can You Find Mohammad's Trusty Friend? The Secrets of the Armenian Garden of Eden. After Whom is Jimmy's Alley in the German Colony Named? Who Taught Sir Moses Montefiore to Build the Flour Mill? Who Dared Replace Jerusalem Stone With Tin Plating? The Oldest Villa in Rehavia. Where Are Prayers Translated into Paintings? The Synagogue Over the Catholic Chapel. What Happens When the Rabbi Dies in the Middle of the War? Who Lives Inside the Israel Museum?

The Mother-In-Law of Elizabeth II, Queen of England, Asked to Be Buried on the Mount of Olives

The Russian church of Mary Magdalene at Gethsemane, at the foot of the Mount of Olives, is best known for its seven round golden cupolas that are reminiscent of the turrets of the Ascension church in Moscow's Kremlin.

The Church of Mary Magdalene, and the monastery contained inside it, belong to the White Russian Church. They were built in 1888 by Czar Alexander III in memory of his mother the Czarina Maria Alexandrova. The church cannot be ignored, owing to its beauty and its position opposite the Old City and, judging by the number of pilgrims and tourists who visit it, the church is known throughout the world.

In addition to all the architectural splendor, the tended garden, large stone rooms and important art treasures (such as a work by Alexander Ivanov, one of the greatest Russian painters of the nineteenth century), there is a magnificent coffin made of burnished gleaming wood, on a dais in one of the small rooms, draped in a flag and covered with fresh flowers.

None of the visitors stops to take a look inside of the room, both because the door is half closed and also because the crypt, although new, is not familiar to many of the visitors here. The visitors would, one presumes, be surprised to learn that this is the final resting place of Princess Alice, the mother-in-law of the current Queen of England, Elizabeth II, who died in 1969 at Buckingham Palace in London.

How did an English princess, whose great-grandmother was none other than Queen Victoria, come to be buried in a faraway country on the edge of the desert? Cynics might suggest that her influential niece, Queen Elizabeth, wanted to keep the princess as far away as possible – as is supposed to be the wish of many a daughter-in-law. But, this is not the case here.

Princess Alice of Battenberg was born in 1885. She was the daughter of Queen Victoria's granddaughter. In 1904, she married Prince Andrew, the son of King George I of Greece, and his wife Queen Olga. The couple had four daughters and a son in Greece, the latter being Prince Phillip, who was later to marry the woman who became Queen Elizabeth II of England.

In 1922, following Greece's military defeat by Turkey, the king and queen and the whole royal household were sent into exile. Princess Alice, her husband and sons found refuge in France, where the princess became a devout Christian. She established various charity organizations to help Greek refugees and joined the Greek Orthodox Church.

During World War II, Alice lived in Athens and, despite the fact that her four daughters were married to German princes, she was a strong opponent of the Germans and even concealed a Jewish family in her home. She was later recognized by Yad Vashem as one of the Righteous among the Nations. The honor was presented to two of her children in Jerusalem, one of whom was Prince Phillip, in 1994. They also visited their mother's grave for the first time.

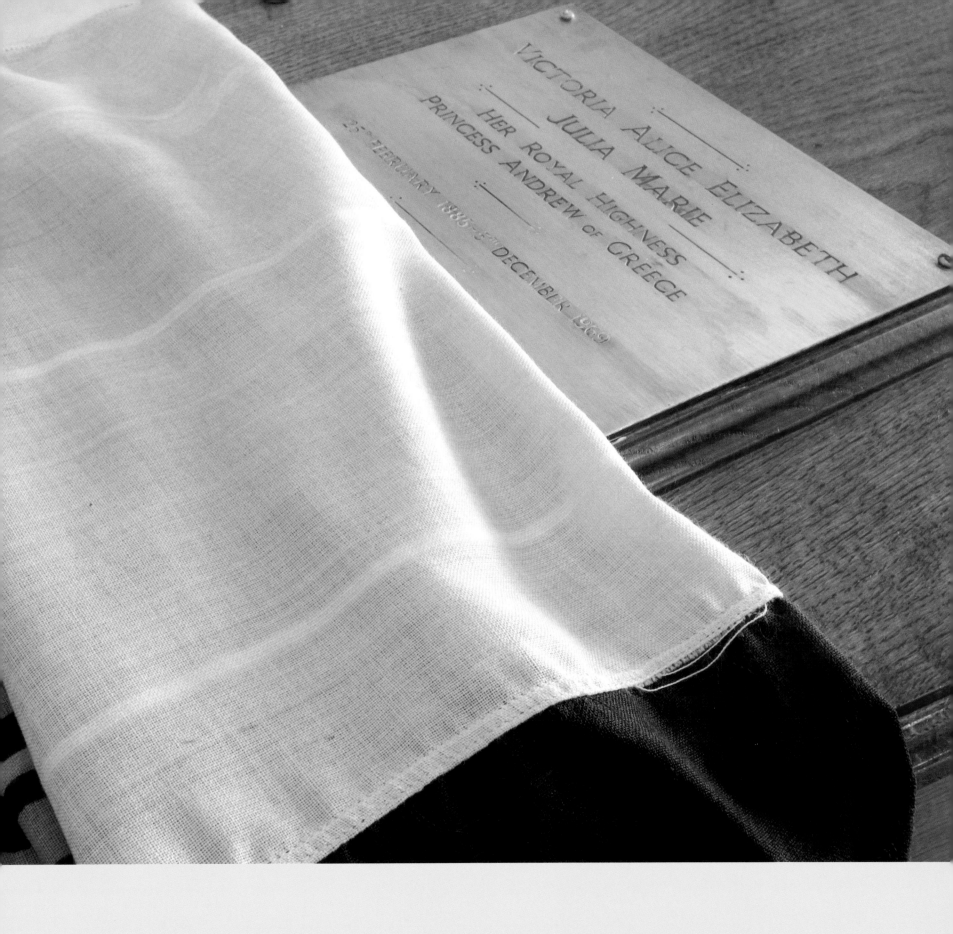

In 1947, Princess Alice returned to England to attend the wedding of her son Phillip to Princess Elizabeth and, in 1948, she joined a Greek Orthodox monastery, moved to the Greek island of Tinos and adopted the life of a nun, despite the fact that she had been married and had given birth to five children.

Princess Alice attended the coronation of her daughter-in-law, Queen Elizabeth, in 1953 dressed unconventionally in the attire of a nun. Before she died, her son brought her to Buckingham Palace where she lived out her remaining years. She died in the palace in 1969 and was buried in the family plot in the church at Windsor Castle. However, she had asked to be buried in the church of Mary Magdalene at Gethsemane alongside her aunt, Elizabeth Fyodorovna, wife of Prince Sergei, brother of the last Russian czar, Alexander III. Her aunt Elizabeth worked tirelessly to establish the church and, when she was executed in 1918, her remains were smuggled out of Russia via China to Jerusalem and she was interred in the church. It was only in 1988 that Alice's remains were brought to Israel and she was buried in the church of Mary Magdalene in Jerusalem.

Thus modestly, but with much splendor and majesty, a real princess, a special character and a Righteous among the Nations, came to be buried here.

The Church of Mary Magdalene, Gethsemane.

Who Founded an African Village on the Roof of the Church of the Holy Sepulcher? What Do the Nuns Do at the Sixth Station? Is this a Synagogue or a Church? What Can You Find on the Second Floor of the Drapery Store? What's on Offer at Antioch's Descendants' Museum? Who is Really Buried in the Architects' Grave at Jaffa Gate? Where Can You Find a Neighborhood Oven to Use? What's on the Bridge Over the Way to the Western Wall? How to Get to Vienna Via the Old City? Why is the English Princess Buried in a Russian Church? **The House Above the Floor of the Armenian Church.** Where Did President Ben-Zvi Find a Quiet Spot? With Whom Did Richard Gere Share the "Fourth Wife's Room"? What Lies Shimmering at the Heart of the Museum? What's Special about Eliyahu's Pita Bread? What is Buddha Doing in a Suburbian House? Who Plays Bowls in the Middle of the Forest? Where Are the Indian Soldiers of His Majesty's Army Buried? What Lurks Near the Entrance to Hell? The Cistern that Became a Hamam, and the Hospital that Became a Hotel. How Much Honor Can the High Commissioner Bestow on the Cat? Who Warmed Themselves by the High Commissioner's Hearth? Is the Gate Crooked or Did the Floor Move? Who Built a White Bench by the Mar Elias Monastery? How Did the Concrete of the Gilo Security Wall become Transparent? Where Did the Animals Go When They Left Noah's Ark? Where Do the Stairs from the Mall Parking Lot Lead? A Work of Art Made to be Walked On. Where is the Brother of the Sundial on Jaffa Road? What Happens at Mahaneh Yehudah Market After the Vegetable Stall Owners Close for the Day? Where is the Entrance to the World's Most Secret Kabbalah Center? Where Did the Greek Patriarch, St. Simon, and Saul Tchernichowski Meet? How Far Were the Limbs of Og, the King of Bashan, Scattered? Where Can You Find Mohammad's Trusty Friend? The Secrets of the Armenian Garden of Eden. After Whom is Jimmy's Alley in the German Colony Named? Who Taught Sir Moses Montefiore to Build the Flour Mill? Who Dared Replace Jerusalem Stone With Tin Plating? The Oldest Villa in Rehavia. Where Are Prayers Translated into Paintings? The Synagogue Over the Catholic Chapel. What Happens When the Rabbi Dies in the Middle of the War? Who Lives Inside the Israel Museum?

A Complete Armenian Mosaic in a House near Damascus Gate

Not far from Damascus Gate, in an area known for its plethora of pita bread bakeries, there is an ordinary looking building at 18 Hanevi'im Street. Inside the building is a small apartment whose floor is made of a spectacular mosaic that has survived intact since the sixth century.

The shock of seeing the splendorous floor is not just a result of its surprising location but also because of the rare condition of all the stones of the mosaic, which covers the entire area. In fact, it looks like the walls were built around, and in honor of, the mosaic, so as not to take anything away from its beauty.

Until recently, the building was used as a residence and the mosaic was used as a regular floor. Even now you can see small cavities at the edges of the mosaic into which water drained, when the floor was washed, and from which the water was collected in jars and disposed of.

The mosaic was originally installed in an Armenian church built in 550 CE. Despite dating back to sixth century, the images in the mosaic seem strangely familiar. They are precisely the same images that appear in Armenian pottery work made today. The motifs were handed down by the community's craftsmen through the generations. Although, today, the pictures appear on pottery jars and not in mosaics, the spectacular peacocks, fruits, and vine tendrils are identical.

At the bottom of the mosaic there is a pitcher – amphora in Greek – with a peacock with a colorful tail on either side. Vine branches with heavy bunches of grapes twist and turn out of the pitcher. The vine tendrils form circles on the floor that contain pictures of pigeons, geese, storks, swallows, pheasants, and other birds. The mosaic also features a picture of a basket with fruit pouring out of it, as a symbol of plenty; a birds' cage symbolizing the human spirit entrapped in the body; a pair of birds facing each other on vine branches; and a grail from which Jesus drank. Above an inscription to the Unknown Soldier is an ornate tray with fruit and a bird on either side of it.

There is an inscription at the top of the mosaic which reads: "To the Memory and Salvation of all Armenians. Our Lord alone Knows their Names." The Armenians believe that the inscription is the first memorial in the world to the Unknown Soldier and that, beneath the floor, is a grave of Armenian soldiers killed in battle. At this stage, the mosaic cannot be viewed as the house is locked, and the key is kept by the Armenian Patriarchate in the Old City. However, assurance has been given that the building will be made suitable for visitors and will be opened to the public because, as the Armenian Patriarchate knows full well, such a work of beauty should not be kept from the world.

18 ha-Nevi'im Street, opposite Damascus Gate.

Who Founded an African Village on the Roof of the Church of the Holy Sepulcher? What Do the Nuns Do at the Sixth Station? Is this a Synagogue or a Church? What Can You Find on the Second Floor of the Drapery Store? What's on Offer at Antioch's Descendants' Museum? Who is Really Buried in the Architects' Grave at Jaffa Gate? Where Can You Find a Neighborhood Oven to Use? What's on the Bridge Over the Way to the Western Wall? How to Get to Vienna Via the Old City? Why is the English Princess Buried in a Russian Church? The House Above the Floor of the Armenian Church. **Where Did President Ben-Zvi Find a Quiet Spot?** With Whom Did Richard Gere Share the "Fourth Wife's Room"? What Lies Shimmering at the Heart of the Museum? What's Special about Eliyahu's Pita Bread? What is Buddha Doing in a Suburbian House? Who Plays Bowls in the Middle of the Forest? Where Are the Indian Soldiers of His Majesty's Army Buried? What Lurks Near the Entrance to Hell? The Cistern that Became a Hamam, and the Hospital that Became a Hotel. How Much Honor Can the High Commissioner Bestow on the Cat? Who Warmed Themselves by the High Commissioner's Hearth? Is the Gate Crooked or Did the Floor Move? Who Built a White Bench by the Mar Elias Monastery? How Did the Concrete of the Gilo Security Wall become Transparent? Where Did the Animals Go When They Left Noah's Ark? Where Do the Stairs from the Mall Parking Lot Lead? A Work of Art Made to be Walked On. Where is the Brother of the Sundial on Jaffa Road? What Happens at Mahaneh Yehudah Market After the Vegetable Stall Owners Close for the Day? Where is the Entrance to the World's Most Secret Kabbalah Center? Where Did the Greek Patriarch, St. Simon, and Saul Tchernichowski Meet? How Far Were the Limbs of Og, the King of Bashan, Scattered? Where Can You Find Mohammad's Trusty Friend? The Secrets of the Armenian Garden of Eden. After Whom is Jimmy's Alley in the German Colony Named? Who Taught Sir Moses Montefiore to Build the Flour Mill? Who Dared Replace Jerusalem Stone With Tin Plating? The Oldest Villa in Rehavia. Where Are Prayers Translated into Paintings? The Synagogue Over the Catholic Chapel. What Happens When the Rabbi Dies in the Middle of the War? Who Lives Inside the Israel Museum?

The President's Room on
the Roof of the World

Between arches and dark corridors the Tomb of David nestles in the darkness, on the ground floor of an old building on Mount Zion. The only light comes from the numerous candles lit by Jews, a custom that has been practiced for hundreds of years. Wax drips everywhere, in the niches between the walls, on the stairs and the stone benches, and imbues the place with a sense of sanctity, of heaviness, and even suffocation. The quiet sobbing and sighing of the worshippers enhances the sense of gloominess that hangs heavily in the dark interior.

Many of the visitors, like their predecessors, light candles, touch the cloth cover of the tomb, and say a prayer. Most don't notice the narrow stairway at the edge of the floor. Those who do, and decide to venture up the stairs, come across a rough lime painted sign that reads "To the President." And then, at the end of the stairs, the world opens up to them.

The large white roof offers an unexpected view. To the east lie the Judean Desert and the Dead Sea and, to the north, a hodgepodge of roofs, of churches and mosques, and the houses of the Old City. There is a small dome in the center of the roof, with a door in the middle that gives you the idea that the dome isn't just there to add to the aesthetics, and that there is a residential purpose to it. This is "the President's room."

Surprisingly, the president in question is not the head of the Sanhedrin (rabbinical high court) or the Great Assembly. The reference is to Israel's first head of state, President Chaim Weizmann. The room on the roof of David's Tomb was granted to Weizmann by the Ministry of Religious Affairs on the occasion of the president's 75th birthday. Two Torah scrolls were also written to mark the event, one was taken to his residence in Rehovot and the other was ceremoniously installed in his "other room" on Mount Zion. The *parokhet* (Torah ark curtain) from the synagogue in the town in which Weizmann was born was also placed there, and thus it officially became "the President's room".

David's Tomb on Mount Zion became a popular site between 1948 and 1967, in the years when Jerusalem was a divided city,

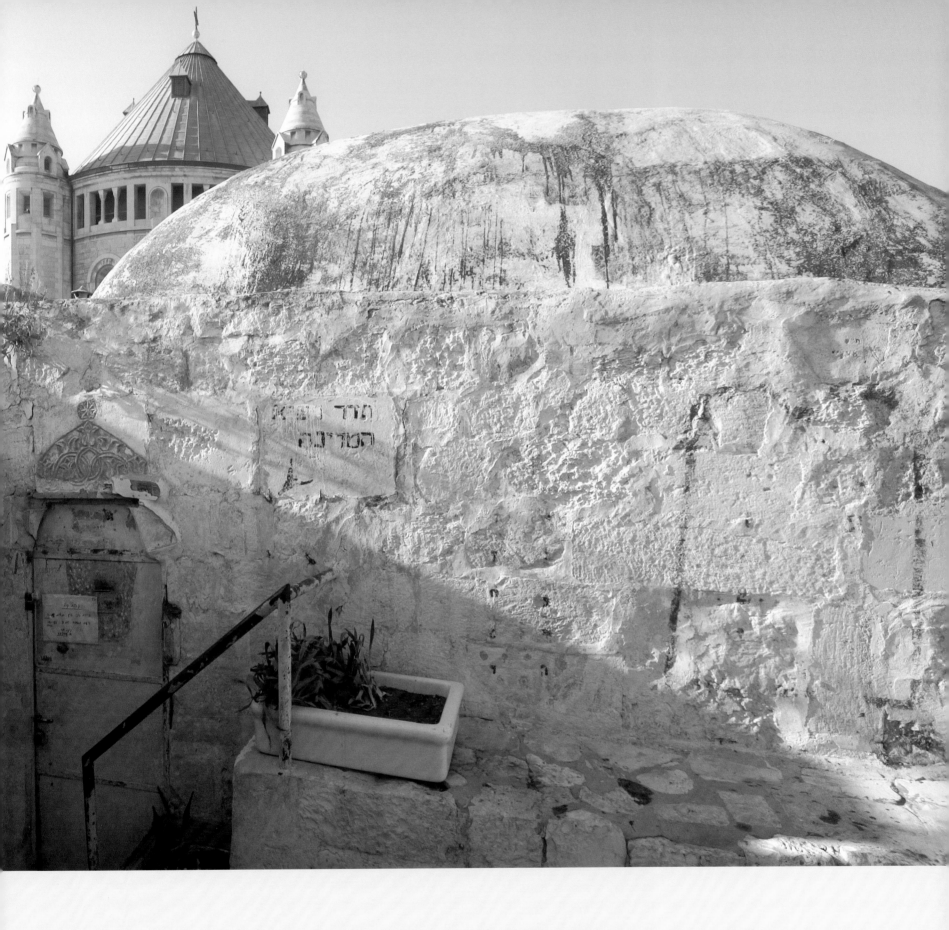

and became one of the main holy places in Israel, not because of its historical significance but due to an existential reality – all the other holy sites were located in the Jordanian-controlled areas. Although the armistice agreement between Israel and Jordan included accord on allowing Jews access to the Western Wall, this was never kept in practice. Jews were prevented from visiting the Western Wall and all the other holy sites in the Old City.

The new situation, the separation of the two parts of the city, forced the Jewish inhabitants to adopt new religious customs suited to the political reality of the day.

The vacuum was filled in a variety of ways. One was the sanctification of David's Tomb on Mount Zion. Although it was clear that David's Tomb was not as important as the Western Wall and other holy places, the fact that it was the only holy site inside the country imbued by tradition with a direct link to the ancient religious history of the Jewish people helped it flourish.

The Ministry of Religious Affairs gave the room above the tomb to the president as it wanted to give the religious site national importance too. Associating the place with the president of the country added state importance to the site and this drew secular visitors, in addition to the many people who went there for religious reasons.

Weizmann, however, who became president at the age of 74, never managed to visit his room there. On the other hand, his successor, Itzhak Ben-Zvi, used to visit the room and look out from the roof, which became known as "the roof observation point," to the eastern and inaccessible part of the city, and to the holy places on the other side of the border, such as the Western Wall and the Mount of Olives. Veterans of the site relate that President Ben-Zvi also used the room for studying and writing.

The room is shut most of the time. However, once a week, between 11 a.m. and 6 p.m. on Mondays, it is opened to the public by an affable man who tells visitors about the room's history, which he learned from his father, who used to study the Talmud with President Ben-Zvi.

The roof of the building of David's Tomb, Mount Zion.

Who Founded an African Village on the Roof of the Church of the Holy Sepulcher? What Do the Nuns Do at the Sixth Station? Is this a Synagogue or a Church? What Can You Find on the Second Floor of the Drapery Store? What's on Offer at Antioch's Descendants' Museum? Who is Really Buried in the Architects' Grave at Jaffa Gate? Where Can You Find a Neighborhood Oven to Use? What's on the Bridge Over the Way to the Western Wall? How to Get to Vienna Via the Old City? Why is the English Princess Buried in a Russian Church? The House Above the Floor of the Armenian Church. Where Did President Ben-Zvi Find a Quiet Spot? With Whom Did Richard Gere Share the "Fourth Wife's Room"? What Lies Shimmering at the Heart of the Museum? What's Special about Eliyahu's Pita Bread? What is Buddha Doing in a Suburbian House? Who Plays Bowls in the Middle of the Forest? Where Are the Indian Soldiers of His Majesty's Army Buried? What Lurks Near the Entrance to Hell? The Cistern that Became a Hamam, and the Hospital that Became a Hotel. How Much Honor Can the High Commissioner Bestow on the Cat? Who Warmed Themselves by the High Commissioner's Hearth? Is the Gate Crooked or Did the Floor Move? Who Built a White Bench by the Mar Elias Monastery? How Did the Concrete of the Gilo Security Wall become Transparent? Where Did the Animals Go When They Left Noah's Ark? Where Do the Stairs from the Mall Parking Lot Lead? A Work of Art Made to be Walked On. Where is the Brother of the Sundial on Jaffa Road? What Happens at Mahaneh Yehudah Market After the Vegetable Stall Owners Close for the Day? Where is the Entrance to the World's Most Secret Kabbalah Center? Where Did the Greek Patriarch, St. Simon, and Saul Tchernichowski Meet? How Far Were the Limbs of Og, the King of Bashan, Scattered? Where Can You Find Mohammad's Trusty Friend? The Secrets of the Armenian Garden of Eden. After Whom is Jimmy's Alley in the German Colony Named? Who Taught Sir Moses Montefiore to Build the Flour Mill? Who Dared Replace Jerusalem Stone With Tin Plating? The Oldest Villa in Rehavia. Where Are Prayers Translated into Paintings? The Synagogue Over the Catholic Chapel. What Happens When the Rabbi Dies in the Middle of the War? Who Lives Inside the Israel Museum?

World Greats, al-Husseini, and the Pilgrims from Chicago at the American Colony

The building, which today houses the American Colony Hotel in the Sheikh Jarrah district, went through numerous changes before it became a luxury hotel.

The term "luxury" doesn't really suit the character of the hotel and doesn't do justice to a hotel with standards of its own. The hotel occupies old buildings. Its rooms are completely different from each other and they are not lined up on either side of corridors but in three buildings. The furniture is not shiny and new but oriental and old. Still, the hotel attracts tourists with refined tastes, journalists and famous media personalities from around the world. Cognoscenti Jerusalemites go to the hotel to bask in the special atmosphere of the central patio. There, seated around tables made of Armenian ceramic tiles, they can sip strong, aromatic Turkish coffee, listen to the water burbling in the fountain, and try to catch a word or two of the Palestinian leaders who go there to discuss world affairs. They can also try to get a glimpse of the interior of the rooms around the water, wondering why the hotel is different from any other in the region.

Of all the extraordinary things in the American Colony Hotel, the most striking of all is Suite no. 6 or, as it is otherwise known, "the Fourth Wife's Room." Few get to see it, or stay in it, as it is the most expensive suite in the hotel. It is mainly used by special guests, like politicians, media persona, and actors (Richard Gere was a recent occupant).

Suite no. 6 was lovingly built by the owner for his fourth, and youngest, wife. Until 1894, the building was the home of Rabbakh Effendi Al-Husseini, a wealthy lawyer who lived there with his three wives. In the winter, they lived on the second floor, and in the summer, they would reside in three rooms on the ground floor around the patio. These were the three wives' summer rooms and the Effendi would rotate between them. When Al-Husseini married his young and beautiful fourth wife, he built a separate wing for her on the east side of the building. She lived in the new, spacious section.

The suite is larger than all other rooms in the house and is composed of a set of rooms. Stairs lead from the entrance area to the room itself, which is large and flooded in light. A small and pretty balcony, with curved iron railings, adjoins the room. There is no hint of how the room was originally furnished but today, the old large flagstones of the floor are covered with heavy oriental carpets, and a pleated colorful cloth canopy hangs down from the ceiling, making the whole room seem like a four poster bed. The rest of the furnishings were collected over time from many eastern countries – Damascene armchairs encrusted with shells, Moroccan footrests, and heavy velvet curtains from India. In the center of the large bathroom is a bath tub that stands on gleaming copper legs, with black and white tiles surrounding it.

After the owner died, his heiresses were forced to rent the house to a group of sixteen fundamentalist American Christians who lived in the Old City of Jerusalem. The Americans, led by Horatio and Anna Spafford, came to Jerusalem in 1881 to live a Spartan religious lifestyle following a series of personal tragedies.

Horatio was a successful lawyer from Chicago. First, his only son died from a serious ailment. Then his house burned down, and his four daughters drowned during a sea voyage to Europe with their mother. The mother survived and, upon her return to America, decided she would not follow those who worshipped God only because He was good to them but rather she would trust in Him so that one day she might gain a better understanding of His ways. According to the husband, the decision to move to Jerusalem was made because "Jerusalem is the place where our Lord suffered and was victorious, and I want to learn how to live, to suffer, and above all, be victorious."

The couple and some of their colleagues arrived in Jerusalem in 1881 and dedicated themselves to charitable work among the Jews and Arabs of the city. In 1894, they were joined by a group of Swedes from America and Sweden and, together, they rented the house and turned it into a farm, bakery, butchery, and photography store. They sold their produce to local residents, were prosperous, and lived a communal lifestyle. The elderly

owner of the hotel, Valentine Vester, who still lives there, claims that this was the first kibbutz in the land.

To boost their revenue, the occupants vacated their rooms during the summer, the time of year when pilgrims came to Jerusalem, and rented out their rooms to the pilgrims. They called this operation the American Colony Hostel.

During World War I, most of the children of the original group left the American colony and the community disbanded. The hotel, however, still belongs to descendants of two of the original group, Spafford and Vester. The hostel operated until 1948, when it was renovated and became a hotel with a special character, which is preserved to this day.

23 Nablus Way, Sheikh Jarrah.

Who Founded an African Village on the Roof of the Church of the Holy Sepulcher? What Do the Nuns Do at the Sixth Station? Is this a Synagogue or a Church? What Can You Find on the Second Floor of the Drapery Store? What's on Offer at Antioch's Descendants' Museum? Who is Really Buried in the Architects' Grave at Jaffa Gate? Where Can You Find a Neighborhood Oven to Use? What's on the Bridge Over the Way to the Western Wall? How to Get to Vienna Via the Old City? Why is the English Princess Buried in a Russian Church? The House Above the Floor of the Armenian Church. Where Did President Ben-Zvi Find a Quiet Spot? With Whom Did Richard Gere Share the "Fourth Wife's Room"?

What Lies Shimmering at the Heart of the Museum? What's Special about Eliyahu's Pita Bread? What is Buddha Doing in a Suburbian House? Who Plays Bowls in the Middle of the Forest? Where Are the Indian Soldiers of His Majesty's Army Buried? What Lurks Near the Entrance to Hell? The Cistern that Became a Hamam, and the Hospital that Became a Hotel. How Much Honor Can the High Commissioner Bestow on the Cat? Who Warmed Themselves by the High Commissioner's Hearth? Is the Gate Crooked or Did the Floor Move? Who Built a White Bench by the Mar Elias Monastery? How Did the Concrete of the Gilo Security Wall become Transparent? Where Did the Animals Go When They Left Noah's Ark? Where Do the Stairs from the Mall Parking Lot Lead? A Work of Art Made to be Walked On. Where is the Brother of the Sundial on Jaffa Road? What Happens at Mahaneh Yehudah Market After the Vegetable Stall Owners Close for the Day? Where is the Entrance to the World's Most Secret Kabbalah Center? Where Did the Greek Patriarch, St. Simon, and Saul Tchernichowski Meet? How Far Were the Limbs of Og, the King of Bashan, Scattered? Where Can You Find Mohammad's Trusty Friend? The Secrets of the Armenian Garden of Eden. After Whom is Jimmy's Alley in the German Colony Named? Who Taught Sir Moses Montefiore to Build the Flour Mill? Who Dared Replace Jerusalem Stone With Tin Plating? The Oldest Villa in Rehavia. Where Are Prayers Translated into Paintings? The Synagogue Over the Catholic Chapel. What Happens When the Rabbi Dies in the Middle of the War? Who Lives Inside the Israel Museum?

The Enchanted Pool of the Rockefeller Museum

Even if the pool is not the most valuable find in the Rockefeller Museum, it is certainly the best concealed find in the compound. The secret pool of the Rockefeller Museum is unusually shaped. It is long and narrow, shaded and surrounded by rich vegetation and elongated stone benches. But it is mostly surrounded by archeological works of art. This is probably why it looks like a large shining diamond embedded in a house of white Jerusalem stone.

The Rockefeller Museum was built during the time of the British Mandate which, although brief, contributed much to Jerusalem's advancement and turned it into a modern city. For the first time since the Crusades it, once again, became the country's capital, and the High Commissioner took up office there. The British administrative offices were established in the city, as were the institutions of the Jewish state in the making that operated alongside the Arab Higher Committee, which represented the Arabs of the Holy Land.

The British built many public institutions in Jerusalem suitable for a modern city – a university, hotels, commercial and office buildings, the High Commissioner's Palace, a post office, a bank and an archeological museum – the Rockefeller Museum.

In order to fund the construction work, they raised a donation of two million dollars from the American mogul John D. Rockefeller Jr. and in 1930, the cornerstone of the museum was laid. The museum was opened to the general public in January 1938.

The design and construction of the building were overseen by architect Austen St. Barbe Harrison. He also designed the High Commissioner's Palace and the main post office on Jaffa Road. Before starting work on the museum, he embarked on a study tour of European cities to examine the famous museums. He concluded that the Jerusalem museum should combine elements from the west with others inspired by ancient eastern cultures.

After his European tour, Harrison spent three months studying architectural elements in the Old City, and these are reflected in the museum doors made of Turkish walnut wood, Armenian ceramic tiles, and stone reliefs made by renowned British artist Eric Gill. Gill carved 11 reliefs in Hebrew, Arabic, and English in the walls of the museum.

The museum itself is the hub of the building although it is built around a central courtyard with the pool in the middle. Special attention was paid to the pool, in the design, despite the fact that it was only planned as a decorative pool.

The pool is surrounded on three sides by arches supported by stone pillars, creating mysterious recesses which house the finds, with works of art displayed over the arches. On either side of the pool there are ten reliefs made by Gill, and there are large stone benches positioned along the length of the pool with low vegetation between them. At one end of the courtyard is a dark and shaded niche, with a canopy of ceramic tiles designed by Armenian artist David Ohanessian.

Since the Six-Day War, the museum has been controlled by Israel and is managed by the Israel Museum. The museum has undergone few changes since it was constructed, and the main displays have remained unchanged. From time to time, there are temporary exhibitions in the secondary exhibition halls.

Because it is located in the east of the city, the museum does not attract many visitors. Few enjoy its beauty and even fewer stop to sit on one of the benches by the secret pool.

The Rockefeller Museum, Sultan Suleiman Street.

78

Who Founded an African Village on the Roof of the Church of the Holy Sepulcher? What Do the Nuns Do at the Sixth Station? Is this a Synagogue or a Church? What Can You Find on the Second Floor of the Drapery Store? What's on Offer at Antioch's Descendants' Museum? Who is Really Buried in the Architects' Grave at Jaffa Gate? Where Can You Find a Neighborhood Oven to Use? What's on the Bridge Over the Way to the Western Wall? How to Get to Vienna Via the Old City? Why is the English Princess Buried in a Russian Church? The House Above the Floor of the Armenian Church. Where Did President Ben-Zvi Find a Quiet Spot? With Whom Did Richard Gere Share the "Fourth Wife's Room"? What Lies Shimmering at the Heart of the Museum? **What's Special about Eliyahu's Pita Bread?** What is Buddha Doing in a Suburban House? Who Plays Bowls in the Middle of the Forest? Where Are the Indian Soldiers of His Majesty's Army Buried? What Lurks Near the Entrance to Hell? The Cistern that Became a Hamam, and the Hospital that Became a Hotel. How Much Honor Can the High Commissioner Bestow on the Cat? Who Warmed Themselves by the High Commissioner's Hearth? Is the Gate Crooked or Did the Floor Move? Who Built a White Bench by the Mar Elias Monastery? How Did the Concrete of the Gilo Security Wall become Transparent? Where Did the Animals Go When They Left Noah's Ark? Where Do the Stairs from the Mall Parking Lot Lead? A Work of Art Made to be Walked On. Where is the Brother of the Sundial on Jaffa Road? What Happens at Mahaneh Yehudah Market After the Vegetable Stall Owners Close for the Day? Where is the Entrance to the World's Most Secret Kabbalah Center? Where Did the Greek Patriarch, St. Simon, and Saul Tchernichowski Meet? How Far Were the Limbs of Og, the King of Bashan, Scattered? Where Can You Find Mohammad's Trusty Friend? The Secrets of the Armenian Garden of Eden. After Whom is Jimmy's Alley in the German Colony Named? Who Taught Sir Moses Montefiore to Build the Flour Mill? Who Dared Replace Jerusalem Stone With Tin Plating? The Oldest Villa in Rehavia. Where Are Prayers Translated into Paintings? The Synagogue Over the Catholic Chapel. What Happens When the Rabbi Dies in the Middle of the War? Who Lives Inside the Israel Museum?

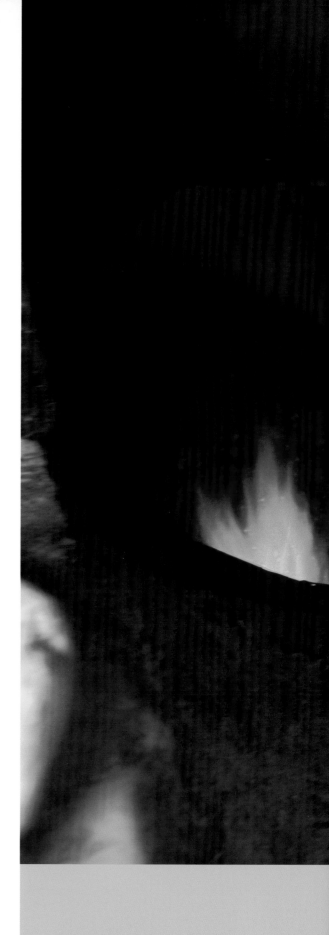

The Last Open Fire Oven

To prepare Iraqi pita bread or, as it is called in Jerusalem, *"pita esh tanoor"* (oven fire pita bread), pita bread that is baked over flames, you need the following ingredients:

  1 kg flour
  50 gr fresh yeast
  2 heaping teaspoonfuls salt
  1 teaspoon sugar
  2.5 cups water

Mix the ingredients together to make soft, uniform, moist dough, let rise, divide into balls of dough and let rise again. Roll out each ball into a round flat shape about half a centimeter (a quarter inch) thick and place on a cloth cushion. Affix the dough firmly to the edges of the cushion and, with practiced action, place the dough on the dome of the oven. The oven's dome shape and the precise heat inside will keep the dough stuck to the dome until it is ready. Then, using long iron tongs, the pita bread can be removed and cast straight into a floured jute sack prepared ahead of time for just this purpose.

Sounds simple and well worth the effort, particularly considering the fruits of your labor – hot and aromatic pita bread, thick at the rim and crusty in the middle. The only problem is, these days, it is hard to find a genuine oven *(taboun)*, made of clay, with flames leaping up inside it and with a round opening that reveals a black cavity with fire inside and dotted with white pita bread dough. It has largely been replaced by modern *taboun*s made of heat absorbing bricks whose color matches the color of the wall.

The modern *taboun* is heated by gas or electricity, and the pita breads come out symmetrical and identical to each other. But there is something missing in the flavor.

In Jerusalem, there is just one *taboun* left from the old generation – Eliyahu's *taboun*, located in the Bukharan Quarter on Yehezkel Street near the Meah She'arim neighborhood. Eliyahu exclusively bakes Iraqi pita bread, from early morning, until he runs out of strength. As the latter never happens at a fixed time of the day, it's best to get there early. You can identify the place by the crowd

gathered outside his "bakery." The bakery is composed of a small room completely taken up by the slightly crooked *taboun* built many years ago by a craftsman who took great care to use the right construction materials, but took less care about making sure the oven was built straight. The first and most important rule for *taboun* construction is that it must be made of clay, which absorbs heat. The second rule is that it should have a dome that is larger and higher than the opening. The rest is of less importance, and a skilled baker like Eliyahu, who has been baking pita bread all his life, will manage. The clay, the heat, and the damp dough guarantee success – these and Eliyahu's internal clock, which tells him exactly when to stop chatting to the customers and climb half way into the taboun to extract the ready pita bread.

Eliyahu has an old sack for the prepared pita bread but he never gets to uses it. The pita breads are snapped up before they hit the sack. This isn't sophisticated food, and not exactly gourmet cooking. But the cognoscenti will know that there is no more exciting sight than a flaming *taboun* packed with pita bread. And there is no pita bread tastier than the ones that come out of Eliyahu's oven.

The Bukharan Market, Yehezkel Street.

Who Founded an African Village on the Roof of the Church of the Holy Sepulcher? What Do the Nuns Do at the Sixth Station? Is this a Synagogue or a Church? What Can You Find on the Second Floor of the Drapery Store? What's on Offer at Antioch's Descendants' Museum? Who is Really Buried in the Architects' Grave at Jaffa Gate? Where Can You Find a Neighborhood Oven to Use? What's on the Bridge Over the Way to the Western Wall? How to Get to Vienna Via the Old City? Why is the English Princess Buried in a Russian Church? The House Above the Floor of the Armenian Church. Where Did President Ben-Zvi Find a Quiet Spot? With Whom Did Richard Gere Share the "Fourth Wife's Room"? What Lies Shimmering at the Heart of the Museum? What's Special about Eliyahu's Pita Bread? **What is Buddha Doing in a Suburbian House?** Who Plays Bowls in the Middle of the Forest? Where Are the Indian Soldiers of His Majesty's Army Buried? What Lurks Near the Entrance to Hell? The Cistern that Became a Hamam, and the Hospital that Became a Hotel. How Much Honor Can the High Commissioner Bestow on the Cat? Who Warmed Themselves by the High Commissioner's Hearth? Is the Gate Crooked or Did the Floor Move? Who Built a White Bench by the Mar Elias Monastery? How Did the Concrete of the Gilo Security Wall become Transparent? Where Did the Animals Go When They Left Noah's Ark? Where Do the Stairs from the Mall Parking Lot Lead? A Work of Art Made to be Walked On. Where is the Brother of the Sundial on Jaffa Road? What Happens at Mahaneh Yehudah Market After the Vegetable Stall Owners Close for the Day? Where is the Entrance to the World's Most Secret Kabbalah Center? Where Did the Greek Patriarch, St. Simon, and Saul Tchernichowski Meet? How Far Were the Limbs of Og, the King of Bashan, Scattered? Where Can You Find Mohammad's Trusty Friend? The Secrets of the Armenian Garden of Eden. After Whom is Jimmy's Alley in the German Colony Named? Who Taught Sir Moses Montefiore to Build the Flour Mill? Who Dared Replace Jerusalem Stone With Tin Plating? The Oldest Villa in Rehavia. Where Are Prayers Translated into Paintings? The Synagogue Over the Catholic Chapel. What Happens When the Rabbi Dies in the Middle of the War? Who Lives Inside the Israel Museum?

A Japanese Garden in Makuya House

The Japanese garden of a seemingly ordinarily looking house at 13 Sheshet ha-Yamim [Six-Day] Street in the Givat ha-Mivtar district is unlike any other garden in the city. The vegetation is different, and the stones are carefully placed in the only place each one could possibly occupy. Everything in the garden is in keeping with a centuries-old tradition.

The house in the special garden is used by officials of the Makuya sect in Israel, and by Japanese students who attend the Hebrew University. It is the hub of the sect's activities in Israel.

The Makuya sect was founded after World War II by Professor Teshima, who came from Kumamoto in south Japan. Teshima was a disciple of the Christian Japanese theologist Uchimura Kanzo, who came to the realization that the roots of Christianity lie in Judaism. This led him to believe that the creation of the State of Israel was part of the realization of the biblical prophecy. This understanding became the basis for the sect's beliefs. Since the 1960s, every member of the sect has added a Hebrew name to his original name and has been sent to Israel to study Hebrew and to work on a kibbutz for a year.

The sect has no religious establishment, and there are no written commandments. Prayers are led by a guide and include many songs – some are taken from the Psalms, some were composed by members of the sect, and some are Israeli songs.

The members of the Makuya sect use a large number of Israeli symbols, such as the seven-branched candelabra and the Israeli flag, and many wear a Star of David. They support the unification of Jerusalem, and make mass pilgrimages at least once a year. These groups hold colorful parades through the streets of Jerusalem and hold ceremonies in the plaza of the Western Wall.

Despite their great admiration for Israeli culture, however, the members of the sect have not forsaken the Japanese Zen garden, even in the heart of Jerusalem. There are many such gardens around the world, but they are all instantly recognizable because they leave no room for improvisation or passing fads, and everything is dictated ahead of time according to strict rules.

Each plant has a role to play, and each stone has a significance of its own. Part of the inspiration for the gardens comes from the unique landscapes found in Japan. Japan is a mountainous country with dramatic views of cliffs, forests, and waterfalls, and weather conditions that are highly changeable. These landscapes, and the atmosphere of mystery that shrouds nature, gave rise to the Shinto religion which is based on respect for, and divinization of, natural phenomena.

Like other pagan traditions, Shinto also believes that all natural phenomena have their own spirit (kami). According to the Shinto religion, the sun possesses a particularly large kami. The sun crosses the world from east to west and, in the Japanese garden, this is reflected by the garden's east-west axis, facing south. The path of the sun across the sky is indicated in the garden by a stream of water that flows from east to west. The water also symbolizes the connection between groups of basic principles, i.e, between the various materials such as boulders, plants, and stones.

The large square stones symbolize Buddhist divinity, which is immovable. The group of rocks in the garden symbolizes Mount Sumaru, and one pool with a small island in the middle symbolizes the Buddhist Garden of Eden. The voyage of the water from its source, at the end of the garden, to the pool at the other end of the path symbolizes the spiritual journey of man leading to enlightenment. Three stones laid in the garden symbolize the three bodies of Buddha, or the triad of man, heaven, and earth.

The Japanese garden is an inseparable part of Buddhist tradition. It is told that, after he lost faith in a life of asceticism, Buddha decided to sit at the foot of a tree in a park in Varanasi, and not move until he achieved enlightenment. After several days of stubborn sitting, and after divesting himself of every layer of the outside world, Buddha reached the enlightenment he sought. He concluded that man must search inwards as enlightenment is contained inside each of us. Concentration and nature are accessories for attaining internal happiness.

Zen scholars concentrated on developing techniques for perceiving and revealing the truth. They believed that truth cannot be conveyed by means of books but only through personal experience and returning to one's earliest experiences. In order to arouse that experience, Zen masters try to generate special stimulation to help students experience meditation and attain enlightenment. In this respect, the Japanese Garden can be perceived as an ecological element that stimulates and encourages meditation.

In its unique order, the Japanese garden expresses the truth of existence, and it comprises something of a scaled down model of nature and all its splendor. All Japanese gardens, big and small, are similar. They all follow the same order of vegetation, and they all have the same significance.

The Makuya Center, 13 Sheshet ha-Yamim Street, Givat ha-Mivtar.

Who Founded an African Village on the Roof of the Church of the Holy Sepulcher? What Do the Nuns Do at the Sixth Station? Is this a Synagogue or a Church? What Can You Find on the Second Floor of the Drapery Store? What's on Offer at Antioch's Descendants' Museum? Who is Really Buried in the Architects' Grave at Jaffa Gate? Where Can You Find a Neighborhood Oven to Use? What's on the Bridge Over the Way to the Western Wall? How to Get to Vienna Via the Old City? Why is the English Princess Buried in a Russian Church? The House Above the Floor of the Armenian Church. Where Did President Ben-Zvi Find a Quiet Spot? With Whom Did Richard Gere Share the "Fourth Wife's Room"? What Lies Shimmering at the Heart of the Museum? What's Special about Eliyahu's Pita Bread? What is Buddha Doing in a Suburbian House?

Who Plays Bowls in the Middle of the Forest? Where Are the Indian Soldiers of His Majesty's Army Buried? What Lurks Near the Entrance to Hell? The Cistern that Became a Hamam, and the Hospital that Became a Hotel. How Much Honor Can the High Commissioner Bestow on the Cat? Who Warmed Themselves by the High Commissioner's Hearth? Is the Gate Crooked or Did the Floor Move? Who Built a White Bench by the Mar Elias Monastery? How Did the Concrete of the Gilo Security Wall become Transparent? Where Did the Animals Go When They Left Noah's Ark? Where Do the Stairs from the Mall Parking Lot Lead? A Work of Art Made to be Walked On. Where is the Brother of the Sundial on Jaffa Road? What Happens at Mahaneh Yehudah Market After the Vegetable Stall Owners Close for the Day? Where is the Entrance to the World's Most Secret Kabbalah Center? Where Did the Greek Patriarch, St. Simon, and Saul Tchernichowski Meet? How Far Were the Limbs of Og, the King of Bashan, Scattered? Where Can You Find Mohammad's Trusty Friend? The Secrets of the Armenian Garden of Eden. After Whom is Jimmy's Alley in the German Colony Named? Who Taught Sir Moses Montefiore to Build the Flour Mill? Who Dared Replace Jerusalem Stone With Tin Plating? The Oldest Villa in Rehavia. Where Are Prayers Translated into Paintings? The Synagogue Over the Catholic Chapel. What Happens When the Rabbi Dies in the Middle of the War? Who Lives Inside the Israel Museum?

The Bowling Green in the Jerusalem Forest

If you stand on one of the peaks of the Jerusalem Hills and look down towards the center of the Jerusalem Forest, you will see something that looks like a giant green billiards table with white balls moving across it.

The picture becomes clearer the nearer you get. The billiards table is, in fact, a well-tended pitch in a clearing in the Jerusalem Forest surrounded by a tightly packed frame of wild pine trees. The white balls are people in white clothes and they roll balls across the pitch. The green baize is actually especially soft grass that has a different shade of green from the vegetation around it. It is smooth and flat and always looks freshly mown.

This is a bowling green that was established in 1989 by a group of immigrants from South Africa and Zimbabwe so that they could take part in their favorite sport, which is popular in their home country.

It is not clear if the founders intended to create such a strong contrast that reflects the difference between their past there and their present lives here, in Jerusalem. However, I believe that there is nothing more surrealistic than watching reserved players conducting themselves in such a disciplined manner on a well-tended green, with a wild forest around them.

This is a sport in which tactics play an all-important role. The players roll the bowls along courses of about 40 meters (about 130 feet). The ball, which weighs two kilograms (approx 4.4 lbs), is made so that one half is heavier than the other so that it follows an elliptical path when rolled.

The captain of the course determines the target at which the bowls are aimed. The captain decides where to place the target and does so based on his knowledge of the particular players and their abilities. If he wishes to make life tough for the players he will place the target far away from the bowlers and if he is feeling generous, he will place it nearer to them.

Many Israelis have now developed a love of the game, and there is also a group of blind people who have joined the club. The visually impaired players are assisted by seeing players, who instruct and guide them during the game.

Games and competitions are held at the bowling green throughout the week and around the year, although blue uniforms are worn in the winter. Dress code is strictly adhered to, and the height of the grass is also closely controlled. Order, discipline, and aesthetics are held in the highest regard.

To reach the bowling green, follow a one-way route that starts at Tzemakh Street and ends at the leisure center in the Jerusalem Forest. Park your car and enter the forest on foot. Follow the sound of bowls crashing into each other.

The Jerusalem Forest near the Haim Tzippori Leisure Center.

Who Founded an African Village on the Roof of the Church of the Holy Sepulcher? What Do the Nuns Do at the Sixth Station? Is this a Synagogue or a Church? What Can You Find on the Second Floor of the Drapery Store? What's on Offer at Antioch's Descendants' Museum? Who is Really Buried in the Architects' Grave at Jaffa Gate? Where Can You Find a Neighborhood Oven to Use? What's on the Bridge Over the Way to the Western Wall? How to Get to Vienna Via the Old City? Why is the English Princess Buried in a Russian Church? The House Above the Floor of the Armenian Church. Where Did President Ben-Zvi Find a Quiet Spot? With Whom Did Richard Gere Share the "Fourth Wife's Room"? What Lies Shimmering at the Heart of the Museum? What's Special about Eliyahu's Pita Bread? What is Buddha Doing in a Suburbian House? Who Plays Bowls in the Middle of the Forest? **Where Are the Indian Soldiers of His Majesty's Army Buried?** What Lurks Near the Entrance to Hell? The Cistern that Became a Hamam, and the Hospital that Became a Hotel. How Much Honor Can the High Commissioner Bestow on the Cat? Who Warmed Themselves by the High Commissioner's Hearth? Is the Gate Crooked or Did the Floor Move? Who Built a White Bench by the Mar Elias Monastery? How Did the Concrete of the Gilo Security Wall become Transparent? Where Did the Animals Go When They Left Noah's Ark? Where Do the Stairs from the Mall Parking Lot Lead? A Work of Art Made to be Walked On. Where is the Brother of the Sundial on Jaffa Road? What Happens at Mahaneh Yehudah Market After the Vegetable Stall Owners Close for the Day? Where is the Entrance to the World's Most Secret Kabbalah Center? Where Did the Greek Patriarch, St. Simon, and Saul Tchernichowski Meet? How Far Were the Limbs of Og, the King of Bashan, Scattered? Where Can You Find Mohammad's Trusty Friend? The Secrets of the Armenian Garden of Eden. After Whom is Jimmy's Alley in the German Colony Named? Who Taught Sir Moses Montefiore to Build the Flour Mill? Who Dared Replace Jerusalem Stone With Tin Plating? The Oldest Villa in Rehavia. Where Are Prayers Translated into Paintings? The Synagogue Over the Catholic Chapel. What Happens When the Rabbi Dies in the Middle of the War? Who Lives Inside the Israel Museum?

A Modest and Concealed Communal Burial Place in Talpiyot

Most of the residents on Korei ha-Dorot Street in the Talpiyot district know nothing about the tidy garden in the middle of their street, near the water tower. When asked about it, they simply shrug their shoulders in complete ignorance. Sometimes they talk in wonderment about how well the spot is kept and the way the locked site is maintained. Indeed, this is a tiny green spot of land where the grass is mown to precision, although there is no sign there explaining the nature of the place.

The mystery is unraveled by the elders of Talpiyot. This is an Indian cemetery with a communal grave of Indian soldiers who fought against Turkey in the World War I as part of the British Army, and died here.

By the end of the war, 1,104,890 soldiers of the British Empire had fallen in foreign lands. The best brains of the empire helped to commemorate these soldiers. The planning was carried out by Sir Patrick Canyouk, the director of the British Museum, and the inscription on the tombs was chosen by the writer and poet, Rudyard Kipling. The architects who built New Delhi were engaged to plan the cemetery and memorial tombs for the fallen, whose final resting place was unknown. None other than Winston Churchill headed the cemeteries committee.

Immediately after the war, it was decided to bury all dead soldiers in the place where they were killed, and not to transfer their remains to a cemetery near their homes. This decision, which was initially explained as dictated by circumstances, became a principle after the war, as all were equal before death. The Empire did not want to give rise to a situation in which the wealthy could transfer their relatives' remains to their homes, while the less well-off remained far away from their loved ones.

Another decision that was made determined that the tombs would not bear a cross or any other religious symbols. Instead they would have a uniform stone, based on the argument that the war unified everyone, regardless of race, color, or beliefs. The chairman of the memorial committee, Winston Churchill, decided that: "The cemeteries will be completely different from standard

94

זכרות זה
חנם
מוות

THE LAND ON WHICH T
GIFT OF THE PEOPLE C
RESTING PLACE OF TH
FELL IN THE WAR OF I

אור

cemeteries which mark the final resting place of those who leave us, each year, in the normal course of human fate... The cemeteries of those who fell in the Great War will be preserved as a living and perfect memorial to the endeavor and glory of the British Army, and to the sacrifice it made for a lofty goal."

There are five British cemeteries in Israel, with 15,100 graves. There are two British military cemeteries in Jerusalem, in Talpiyot and on Mount Scopus. The one on Mount Scopus is, without doubt, the most impressive due to its position, and it became the main memorial site in pre-statehood Israel. It was also chosen to commemorate the 3,366 British soldiers killed in Palestine and Egypt whose burial place is unknown.

The cemetery on Mount Scopus was planned in accordance with the principles laid down by the British memorial committee: uniform gravestones, a chapel containing a list of the fallen and the missing who fell in Palestine, and a memorial tombstone for those whose final resting place is unknown. The cemetery layout is designed like "an English garden," with lawns and low sculptures.

The brotherhood of warriors, however, which was commemorated so impressively at the Mount Scopus cemetery, was unfortunately not maintained at the Indian cemetery. The soldiers of the Indian Army, who initially served in units in France and were then transferred to Iraq and ended World War I in Palestine, did not find their final resting place alongside their British comrades. They were placed elsewhere in Jerusalem, far away from Mount Scopus, in the district of Talpiyot.

The site was originally used to bury 290 Turkish soldiers, in a communal grave, during the World War I. Between July 1918 and June 1920 two communal graves were sited nearby, without the soldiers' names – one with 31 Muslim soldiers and another with 47 Hindi, Sikh, and Gurkha soldiers.

After the end of the war, when the British wanted to re-inter the fallen who had been hurriedly buried and move them to the military cemetery, they encountered some special problems resulting from Indian customs. The Muslims prohibit the reopening of graves for reburial while the Hindis cremate their dead. It was also difficult to identify the fallen as the Indian military authorities did not maintain a comprehensive registration system.

Owing to the situation and conditions the memorial committee had no choice but to leave the situation unchanged, and to construct two identical memorial tombstones – one for the Muslim soldiers bearing a verse from the Koran, and the other for the Hindi, Sikh, and Gurkha soldiers with an inscription in Sanskrit. The soldiers' names are listed together and kept in the chapel on Mount Scopus.

In contrast to the Mount Scopus cemetery where memorial services were held, and relatives went to visit the graves of their loved ones, there are no visitors to the Indian cemetery, and no family members of the fallen come to Israel from India to lay a wreath on their graves.

But despite the anonymity of the Indian cemetery, it has not been forgotten. It is wonderfully tended. And, despite its small size, its impressive tombstones and beauty fill passers-by with amazement and provide a worthy resting place for its residents.

Kore ha-Dorot Street, Talpiyot.

Who Founded an African Village on the Roof of the Church of the Holy Sepulcher? What Do the Nuns Do at the Sixth Station? Is this a Synagogue or a Church? What Can You Find on the Second Floor of the Drapery Store? What's on Offer at Antioch's Descendants' Museum? Who is Really Buried in the Architects' Grave at Jaffa Gate? Where Can You Find a Neighborhood Oven to Use? What's on the Bridge Over the Way to the Western Wall? How to Get to Vienna Via the Old City? Why is the English Princess Buried in a Russian Church? The House Above the Floor of the Armenian Church. Where Did President Ben-Zvi Find a Quiet Spot? With Whom Did Richard Gere Share the "Fourth Wife's Room"? What Lies Shimmering at the Heart of the Museum? What's Special about Eliyahu's Pita Bread? What is Buddha Doing in a Suburbian House? Who Plays Bowls in the Middle of the Forest? Where Are the Indian Soldiers of His Majesty's Army Buried? **What Lurks Near the Entrance to Hell?** The Cistern that Became a Hamam, and the Hospital that Became a Hotel. How Much Honor Can the High Commissioner Bestow on the Cat? Who Warmed Themselves by the High Commissioner's Hearth? Is the Gate Crooked or Did the Floor Move? Who Built a White Bench by the Mar Elias Monastery? How Did the Concrete of the Gilo Security Wall become Transparent? Where Did the Animals Go When They Left Noah's Ark? Where Do the Stairs from the Mall Parking Lot Lead? A Work of Art Made to be Walked On. Where is the Brother of the Sundial on Jaffa Road? What Happens at Mahaneh Yehudah Market After the Vegetable Stall Owners Close for the Day? Where is the Entrance to the World's Most Secret Kabbalah Center? Where Did the Greek Patriarch, St. Simon, and Saul Tchernichowski Meet? How Far Were the Limbs of Og, the King of Bashan, Scattered? Where Can You Find Mohammad's Trusty Friend? The Secrets of the Armenian Garden of Eden. After Whom is Jimmy's Alley in the German Colony Named? Who Taught Sir Moses Montefiore to Build the Flour Mill? Who Dared Replace Jerusalem Stone With Tin Plating? The Oldest Villa in Rehavia. Where Are Prayers Translated into Paintings? The Synagogue Over the Catholic Chapel. What Happens When the Rabbi Dies in the Middle of the War? Who Lives Inside the Israel Museum?

Illuminated Burial Caves at the Edge of Ben-Hinom Valley

Twenty years ago, a genuine and valuable treasure was discovered opposite the Jerusalem Cinematheque, near the Begin Heritage Center on Derekh Hevron [Hebron Way], that was well concealed in the rock.

The find was seven burial caves from the First Temple era that contained a treasure of silver jewelry, earthenware vessels, glass jars, needles, arrowheads, makeup sticks, gold rings and earrings. All attest to the wealth and fine taste of those who were buried there.

The centerpiece of the whole treasure trove is two wafer-thin silver tablets that are rolled up like two tiny scrolls that bear the priests' benediction: "The Lord bless thee, and keep thee. The Lord make his face shine upon thee, and be gracious unto thee. The Lord lift up his countenance upon thee, and give thee peace" (Num. 6:24–26). The tablets were worn around the neck like an amulet. The importance of this find lies not only in the fact that this is the earliest archeological find anywhere with a biblical inscription – it dates to the sixth or seventh century BCE – but also because, if they were worn around the neck, wearing an artifact with verses from the Torah represents the beginning of the custom of using phylacteries.

The seven First Temple era caves and the Jerusalem Cinematheque stand opposite each other at the entrance of the Valley of Hinnom, or its ancient name of Gei Ben-Hinnom (the Valley of Ben-Hinnom), facing Mount Zion and the wall of the Old City. The spot received a violent sounding name because during the First Temple period, it was used as a cult site to the god Moloch, which included a rite that involved sacrificing children to Moloch and burning them alive. Because of the atrocities committed there, the name Gei Ben-Hinnom took on another meaning, besides its geographical significance, of abstract religious importance. "Gehinnom" became synonymous with hell. The rabbinical Sages described the place as follows: "There are two pillars of fire in Gei Ben-Hinnom, and smoke rises between them… and this is the entrance to gehinnom" (Babylonian Talmud, Sukkah 32b).

Owing to the nature of the place, it was used as a burial ground for residents of Jerusalem of the time. Some burials took place in caves hewn out of the rock and were probably used to bury members of royal families, and of the wealthy, while the others were buried in ordinary graves.

The burial caves near the Cinematheque became known as "the Hinnom shoulder," a name randomly given to them by archeologist Dr. Gabriel Barkai, who discovered them during excavations that took place there between 1975 and 1994, as the boundary between the territories of Judea and Benjamin passed through "the Jebusite shoulder", which is after "Gei Ben-Hinnom".

Burial shelves were hewn in each of the caves on which the bodies of the departed were laid in a supine position. In some caves, pillow-like raised shapes were hewn into the stone, with headrests and an opening for the neck sculpted into them. In addition, oil lamps, food and drink utensils, personal items, and jewelry were placed next to the body. The image provided by the special design of the burial caves is that, in those days, death was considered a sort of prolonged slumber in a carved stone bed.

Some of the caves acted as a family burial estate for many generations. So here, in the same cave, a grandfather, grandson, and great-grandson were all buried, and each generation knew that, when their time came, they would join them there. When all the burial shelves in a cave were occupied by the dead, some of the bones were gathered and transferred for secondary burial in a special repository (*"ma'aseffa"* in Hebrew) hewn into the floor of the cave.

The term used in the Scriptures to describe death is *"ne'esaff"* (gathered): "Behold therefore, I will gather thee unto thy fathers, and thou shalt be gathered into thy grave in peace" (2 Kings 22:20). It seems the term "gathered" describes the placing of the body in the cave, whereas the second stage, in which the bones are placed in the repository, is called burial. The repository of one of the graves contained the remains of 95 people. Part of the incredible treasure found in the caves is now displayed in the Israel Museum.

On the other hand, you don't have to go to the museum to see the caves. All you have to do is cross the cinematheque street and take a good look. The best time to view them is in the late afternoon when the rays of the sun shine into them and illuminate them, or late at night when a concealed candle lights them up from the inside. That is also the best time to catch a movie.

11 Derekh Hevron [Hebron Way], opposite the Jerusalem Cinematheque.

Who Founded an African Village on the Roof of the Church of the Holy Sepulcher? What Do the Nuns Do at the Sixth Station? Is this a Synagogue or a Church? What Can You Find on the Second Floor of the Drapery Store? What's on Offer at Antioch's Descendants' Museum? Who is Really Buried in the Architects' Grave at Jaffa Gate? Where Can You Find a Neighborhood Oven to Use? What's on the Bridge Over the Way to the Western Wall? How to Get to Vienna Via the Old City? Why is the English Princess Buried in a Russian Church? The House Above the Floor of the Armenian Church. Where Did President Ben-Zvi Find a Quiet Spot? With Whom Did Richard Gere Share the "Fourth Wife's Room"? What Lies Shimmering at the Heart of the Museum? What's Special about Eliyahu's Pita Bread? What is Buddha Doing in a Suburbian House? Who Plays Bowls in the Middle of the Forest? Where Are the Indian Soldiers of His Majesty's Army Buried? What Lurks Near the Entrance to Hell? **The Cistern that Became a Hamam, and the Hospital that Became a Hotel.** How Much Honor Can the High Commissioner Bestow on the Cat? Who Warmed Themselves by the High Commissioner's Hearth? Is the Gate Crooked or Did the Floor Move? Who Built a White Bench by the Mar Elias Monastery? How Did the Concrete of the Gilo Security Wall become Transparent? Where Did the Animals Go When They Left Noah's Ark? Where Do the Stairs from the Mall Parking Lot Lead? A Work of Art Made to be Walked On. Where is the Brother of the Sundial on Jaffa Road? What Happens at Mahaneh Yehudah Market After the Vegetable Stall Owners Close for the Day? Where is the Entrance to the World's Most Secret Kabbalah Center? Where Did the Greek Patriarch, St. Simon, and Saul Tchernichowski Meet? How Far Were the Limbs of Og, the King of Bashan, Scattered? Where Can You Find Mohammad's Trusty Friend? The Secrets of the Armenian Garden of Eden. After Whom is Jimmy's Alley in the German Colony Named? Who Taught Sir Moses Montefiore to Build the Flour Mill? Who Dared Replace Jerusalem Stone With Tin Plating? The Oldest Villa in Rehavia. Where Are Prayers Translated into Paintings? The Synagogue Over the Catholic Chapel. What Happens When the Rabbi Dies in the Middle of the War? Who Lives Inside the Israel Museum?

The Renovated Turkish Bath in the Mount Zion Hotel

Any Israeli tourist to Turkey makes sure he or she includes a visit to a genuine Turkish bathhouse while they are there. They bask in an ancient practice, knowing that the Turkish bath, that dark and steamy establishment, has all but disappeared from their home country.

The bathhouse, or *hammam*, which originates in the Roman and Byzantine culture, developed in Islamic society owing to religious laws governing bodily cleanliness. Ceremonies are held for brides and grooms on their wedding day, and for babies when they are 40 days old. But it also serves the location of a ceremony of no lesser importance: for meetings of a social and non-obligatory nature, as men and women use the *hammam* on different days, or at different times of the day. This allows the patrons to behave freely with the bathhouse becoming the center of their social lives.

In Jerusalem too, Turkish bathhouses were very common and played a major role in the social life of both Jews and Arabs. Today, there is evidence of the existence of four bathhouses from those days that were frequented on the eves of religious holidays, used by brides and grooms the night before their wedding. As bathrooms and showers were not a common phenomenon in houses back then, people would visit bathhouses just to get clean. That's where the basic rules of hygiene were learned – a sort of early school for beauty care.

Researcher Yeshayahu Press, in one of his papers, describes the Jerusalem bathhouse as follows: "When you enter the bathhouse you find yourself in a large hall with a round dome about 4–5 meters [13–16.4 ft] high. The rooms for washing are sealed and there are round ventilation holes in the domes above them. There is a small pool in the floor next to all the walls, with hot water running into the pools through a hole in the wall. The bather sits on the stone floor next to the pool, draws water out of it with a tin utensil, pours water over himself and washes himself with soap. He sits there on the stone shelf for a few moments, and absorbs the steam until the bathhouse attendant arrives...."

Although the above bathhouse was built in the nineteenth century, from its description, it appears to be exactly the same as the old-new Turkish bathhouse at the Mount Zion Hotel on Derekh Hevron [Hebron Way], even though the round holes in the ceiling are now ornate windows, and the holes in the walls are now taps for hot and cold water. However, the dome-shaped structure, the stones shelves, and the thick steam that creates a murky mysterious atmosphere are exactly the same. The *hammam,* which served the Turks either as a bathhouse or as a cistern, today works as a genuine bathhouse unparalleled anywhere else in Israel.

The Mount Zion Hotel, near the Cinematheque, does not have the appearance of a hotel. That is because it was originally built as an eye hospital that opened in 1882 at the initiative of the Duke of Kent, Knight of the Order of St. John. When the Duke visited Jerusalem, he decided the best way to be of service to the city was to establish a hospital that would treat eye ailments.

When the War of Independence broke out in 1948, the hospital was abandoned and Haganah soldiers used the building as a stronghold. Later, when Haganah forces took over Mount Zion, a situation arose in which the Ben-Hinnom Valley between Mount Zion and the hospital was exposed to Jordanian shelling. This made the transfer of ammunition and wounded soldiers across the valley impossible. This produced an unusual engineering invention – a cable car from the hospital building to Mount Zion. A thick steel cable was strung across the valley and, during the day, was lowered to the ground so as not to attract the attention of the Arab legion soldiers stationed on the walls of the Old City. The cable was raised again at night and the improvised cable car, which had only one car, worked for about six months. It was used to transfer reinforcement materials, equipment, and ammunition to Mount Zion, and to take the wounded and dead the other way.

For a period of nineteen years, between the War of Independence and the Six-Day War, the area was off the beaten track. Even so, students of the Hebrew University lived in the old hospital building.

In 1986, the Mount Zion Hotel was opened and now operates out of the old hospital buildings that were carefully renovated and restored. The cable car system was also renovated and there is even a cable car museum.

Mount Zion Hotel – 17 Derekh Hevron [Hebron Way].

Who Founded an African Village on the Roof of the Church of the Holy Sepulcher? What Do the Nuns Do at the Sixth Station? Is this a Synagogue or a Church? What Can You Find on the Second Floor of the Drapery Store? What's on Offer at Antioch's Descendants' Museum? Who is Really Buried in the Architects' Grave at Jaffa Gate? Where Can You Find a Neighborhood Oven to Use? What's on the Bridge Over the Way to the Western Wall? How to Get to Vienna Via the Old City? Why is the English Princess Buried in a Russian Church? The House Above the Floor of the Armenian Church. Where Did President Ben-Zvi Find a Quiet Spot? With Whom Did Richard Gere Share the "Fourth Wife's Room"? What Lies Shimmering at the Heart of the Museum? What's Special about Eliyahu's Pita Bread? What is Buddha Doing in a Suburbian House? Who Plays Bowls in the Middle of the Forest? Where Are the Indian Soldiers of His Majesty's Army Buried? What Lurks Near the Entrance to Hell? The Cistern that Became a Hamam, and the Hospital that Became a Hotel.

How Much Honor Can the High Commissioner Bestow on the Cat?

Who Warmed Themselves by the High Commissioner's Hearth? Is the Gate Crooked or Did the Floor Move? Who Built a White Bench by the Mar Elias Monastery? How Did the Concrete of the Gilo Security Wall become Transparent? Where Did the Animals Go When They Left Noah's Ark? Where Do the Stairs from the Mall Parking Lot Lead? A Work of Art Made to be Walked On. Where is the Brother of the Sundial on Jaffa Road? What Happens at Mahaneh Yehudah Market After the Vegetable Stall Owners Close for the Day? Where is the Entrance to the World's Most Secret Kabbalah Center? Where Did the Greek Patriarch, St. Simon, and Saul Tchernichowski Meet? How Far Were the Limbs of Og, the King of Bashan, Scattered? Where Can You Find Mohammad's Trusty Friend? The Secrets of the Armenian Garden of Eden. After Whom is Jimmy's Alley in the German Colony Named? Who Taught Sir Moses Montefiore to Build the Flour Mill? Who Dared Replace Jerusalem Stone With Tin Plating? The Oldest Villa in Rehavia. Where Are Prayers Translated into Paintings? The Synagogue Over the Catholic Chapel. What Happens When the Rabbi Dies in the Middle of the War? Who Lives Inside the Israel Museum?

In Memory of Phyllis the High Commissioner's Cat

As in many old cemeteries, here, too, there are smashed, bent tombstones toppling over. Small stones lie scattered on the ground and, in the rainy months, moss covers the writing inscribed on the stone. The place is arid in the summer – it is right on the edge of the desert. The tombstones are somewhat smaller than usual and look strange. They are the size of small pillows, raised a little above the ground, and the inscriptions on them fill up the entire area of the stone.

The location of the cemetery is also curious – in the middle of the garden of the High Commissioner's Palace (or Residence; in Hebrew. Armon ha-Natziv) in Talpiyyot and very close to the building. Visitors to the spot can enjoy a breathtaking view of the desert from the small hill.

When you get close enough to be able to make out the writing on the stones, you discover that the interred are none other than the beloved pets of the residents of the High Commissioner's Palace over the years, from the dog of the High Commissioner's secretary to Phyllis the cat, who was the pet of one of the UN soldiers who served at the compound a few years ago.

The magnificent palace occupies one of the most beautiful spots in Jerusalem, offering a wonderful view of the Old City, which lies stretched out like a landscape painting. The palace also overlooks Mount Moriah, the Kidron Valley, the Mount of Olives, Mount Scopus, the Judean Desert, the Dead Sea, and the Jordan Valley. The animal cemetery also occupies the choicest spot on the residence grounds. The planners evidently not only loved animals, they also wanted to provide them with an honorable final resting place. The animals ended up with a grave with a view of the holiest spot on Earth, close to the Mount of Olives, a place to which many aspire, where they buy a burial plot and pray daily that they may find their final resting place there. Here, of all places, cats and dogs that were lucky enough to belong to people with the greatest of respect for their pets, are buried.

The garden of the High Commissioner's Palace, East Talpiyot.

Who Founded an African Village on the Roof of the Church of the Holy Sepulcher? What Do the Nuns Do at the Sixth Station? Is this a Synagogue or a Church? What Can You Find on the Second Floor of the Drapery Store? What's on Offer at Antioch's Descendants' Museum? Who is Really Buried in the Architects' Grave at Jaffa Gate? Where Can You Find a Neighborhood Oven to Use? What's on the Bridge Over the Way to the Western Wall? How to Get to Vienna Via the Old City? Why is the English Princess Buried in a Russian Church? The House Above the Floor of the Armenian Church. Where Did President Ben-Zvi Find a Quiet Spot? With Whom Did Richard Gere Share the "Fourth Wife's Room"? What Lies Shimmering at the Heart of the Museum? What's Special about Eliyahu's Pita Bread? What is Buddha Doing in a Suburbian House? Who Plays Bowls in the Middle of the Forest? Where Are the Indian Soldiers of His Majesty's Army Buried? What Lurks Near the Entrance to Hell? The Cistern that Became a Hamam, and the Hospital that Became a Hotel. How Much Honor Can the High Commissioner Bestow on the Cat? Who Warmed Themselves by the High Commissioner's Hearth? Is the Gate Crooked or Did the Floor Move? Who Built a White Bench by the Mar Elias Monastery? How Did the Concrete of the Gilo Security Wall become Transparent? Where Did the Animals Go When They Left Noah's Ark? Where Do the Stairs from the Mall Parking Lot Lead? A Work of Art Made to be Walked On. Where is the Brother of the Sundial on Jaffa Road? What Happens at Mahaneh Yehudah Market After the Vegetable Stall Owners Close for the Day? Where is the Entrance to the World's Most Secret Kabbalah Center? Where Did the Greek Patriarch, St. Simon, and Saul Tchernichowski Meet? How Far Were the Limbs of Og, the King of Bashan, Scattered? Where Can You Find Mohammad's Trusty Friend? The Secrets of the Armenian Garden of Eden. After Whom is Jimmy's Alley in the German Colony Named? Who Taught Sir Moses Montefiore to Build the Flour Mill? Who Dared Replace Jerusalem Stone With Tin Plating? The Oldest Villa in Rehavia. Where Are Prayers Translated into Paintings? The Synagogue Over the Catholic Chapel. What Happens When the Rabbi Dies in the Middle of the War? Who Lives Inside the Israel Museum?

The Ballroom at the High Commissioner's Palace

Anyone who has read Amos Oz's book *The Hill of Evil Counsel* cannot help but imagine the palace of the High Commissioner in Talpiyot. It was there that romantic balls were held, and where the most important and elegant people in Jerusalem were invited during the British Mandate.

In the summer, tea parties and balls were held in the palace gardens and, in the winter, events were held in the drawing room. The garden and drawing room were specifically designed to host such events in as festive an atmosphere as possible. With this in mind, the designer paid great attention to detail. For example, the wall around the garden was raised to prevent the fierce winds of Talpiyot from billowing the ladies dresses or blowing their hats away and, in the drawing room, a large beautiful hearth was built to keep the large hall warm in winter.

Today, with the palace serving as the headquarters of the UN, balls and festive dinners are no longer held there. Yet, because of the hustle and bustle there, the UN soldiers who fill the place in their colorful uniforms and the melee of languages one hears everywhere, the whole building, and the hearth in particular, look like the last vestiges of a lost era.

The oversized scale and amazing colorfulness of the hearth dominate the entire drawing room and lend the hall an unusual appearance. The hearth, a work of art that was especially commissioned from Armenian craftsman David Ohanessian, is overlain with tiles in various shades of blue containing early Christian motifs found in ancient mosaics in Israel and Jordan, and in a mosaic in the Hisham Palace in Jericho. In this work, as in others, Ohanessian created a unique language that reflects his world, a world with a Christian-Armenian and Jerusalem identity.

The hearth was, naturally, designed to provide heat but it also lends the English-style room something of an eastern character. This is a combination that can only be found in British Mandate architecture in the Middle East.

The High Commissioner's Palace in Jerusalem was designed by architect Austen St. Barbe Harrison, who was the chief architect of the Public Works Department of the British Mandate administration during the 1930s. In his designs, Harrison combined local eastern elements with European elements, and it was he who brought the Armenian artist to the palace.

The palace was built for British High Commissioner Sir Arthur Wauchope, who was stationed in Jerusalem between 1931 and 1938, and for the three high commissioners who succeeded him – Harold MacMichael, John Gort (Lord Gort), and Alan Cunningham. All told, this magnificent building was used by the British for just seventeen years. When the British left Palestine, the building was handed over to the Red Cross delegation, and it, in turn, passed the building on to the UN observers in September 1948.

Today, although the building no longer hosts the city's residents and the sounds of Scottish bands are no longer heard there, it stands as strong and as beautiful as ever, on a hill overlooking the whole of southern Jerusalem.

The hill is also called the Hill of Evil Counsel. According to Christian legend, the hill was the site of the summer house of the high priest of the Temple in the days when Jesus walked through Jerusalem and expressed his – at least to the priests – revolutionary ideas. It was in the high priest's house that the Council of Priests met and decided to hand Jesus over to the Romans. In this way, they hoped to rid themselves of a radical man who was undermining the foundations of the Jewish faith. This counsel – from the point of view of Jewish history – turned out to be bad counsel as, after the Romans crucified Jesus, he became a saint and the damage suffered by the Jewish religion was far greater than the damage that would have been caused by a single individual walking around Jerusalem preaching other ideas.

The High Commissioner's Palace, East Talpiyot.

Who Founded an African Village on the Roof of the Church of the Holy Sepulcher? What Do the Nuns Do at the Sixth Station? Is this a Synagogue or a Church? What Can You Find on the Second Floor of the Drapery Store? What's on Offer at Antioch's Descendants' Museum? Who is Really Buried in the Architects' Grave at Jaffa Gate? Where Can You Find a Neighborhood Oven to Use? What's on the Bridge Over the Way to the Western Wall? How to Get to Vienna Via the Old City? Why is the English Princess Buried in a Russian Church? The House Above the Floor of the Armenian Church. Where Did President Ben-Zvi Find a Quiet Spot? With Whom Did Richard Gere Share the "Fourth Wife's Room"? What Lies Shimmering at the Heart of the Museum? What's Special about Eliyahu's Pita Bread? What is Buddha Doing in a Suburbian House? Who Plays Bowls in the Middle of the Forest? Where Are the Indian Soldiers of His Majesty's Army Buried? What Lurks Near the Entrance to Hell? The Cistern that Became a Hamam, and the Hospital that Became a Hotel. How Much Honor Can the High Commissioner Bestow on the Cat? Who Warmed Themselves by the High Commissioner's Hearth? Is the Gate Crooked or Did the Floor Move? Who Built a White Bench by the Mar Elias Monastery? How Did the Concrete of the Gilo Security Wall become Transparent? Where Did the Animals Go When They Left Noah's Ark? Where Do the Stairs from the Mall Parking Lot Lead? A Work of Art Made to be Walked On. Where is the Brother of the Sundial on Jaffa Road? What Happens at Mahaneh Yehudah Market After the Vegetable Stall Owners Close for the Day? Where is the Entrance to the World's Most Secret Kabbalah Center? Where Did the Greek Patriarch, St. Simon, and Saul Tchernichowski Meet? How Far Were the Limbs of Og, the King of Bashan, Scattered? Where Can You Find Mohammad's Trusty Friend? The Secrets of the Armenian Garden of Eden. After Whom is Jimmy's Alley in the German Colony Named? Who Taught Sir Moses Montefiore to Build the Flour Mill? Who Dared Replace Jerusalem Stone With Tin Plating? The Oldest Villa in Rehavia. Where Are Prayers Translated into Paintings? The Synagogue Over the Catholic Chapel. What Happens When the Rabbi Dies in the Middle of the War? Who Lives Inside the Israel Museum?

The Deceptive Gate in the Wall

Deir Abu-Tor, also known as Hananya Hill, is seemingly just another archeological site, like many others in the Jerusalem area. The site is on a hill at the top of Aminadav Street near Derekh Hevron [Hebron Way], in the heart of the Abu-Tor district. Remnants of a Byzantine church were found in the middle of the site, and there is a wild garden overlooking a spectacular view of the gold and silver domes of the Old City. The garden serves as a sort of buffer zone between the beautifully built neighborhood and the ruins of the church.

The remains of the church, and the garden around it, are not a secret but the gate that leads to them is a great secret, so great in fact that experts and professionals have a hard time fathoming it to this day.

The high stone wall and gate, which is also high, are made of Jerusalem stone and the archeologists believe them to be a late addition, as both were built after 1700. This may be the reason why no one investigated them before now.

The lintel of the gate is made of hewn stone topped by a high arch, and it is seemingly just another Jerusalem gate. But, it is only when you push the creaking iron door open and step through it that you get a sense of unease, as if you lose your sense of balance. It is as if you have stepped into a maze that looks like it goes straight but, in fact, leads off to the side. For a moment, it is unclear whether it is the gate that is not straight, or it is the floor that has moved.

After you repeat the action several times, you begin to realize that the gate is intentionally crooked. It has not subsided or bent with time but, for some unknown reason, was built at an angle. Why did the eighteenth-century architects choose to build a crooked gate to protect the church?

It is unlikely that the design of the gate indicates the sense of humor of the Byzantine priests. Maybe the reason lies in the fact that the gate forces visitors to step to their right as they pass through it, in order to catch sight of some view or a building that has not survived. Another theory proffered by archeologists and architects who examined the ruins there is that the only access route to the church was through bent winding path, and the gate was built that way in order to match the pathway. Who knows? Maybe, in those days, it was easier to put up a bent gate than to straighten out the path.

Aminadav Street, Abu-Tor.

Who Founded an African Village on the Roof of the Church of the Holy Sepulcher? What Do the Nuns Do at the Sixth Station? Is this a Synagogue or a Church? What Can You Find on the Second Floor of the Drapery Store? What's on Offer at Antioch's Descendants' Museum? Who is Really Buried in the Architects' Grave at Jaffa Gate? Where Can You Find a Neighborhood Oven to Use? What's on the Bridge Over the Way to the Western Wall? How to Get to Vienna Via the Old City? Why is the English Princess Buried in a Russian Church? The House Above the Floor of the Armenian Church. Where Did President Ben-Zvi Find a Quiet Spot? With Whom Did Richard Gere Share the "Fourth Wife's Room"? What Lies Shimmering at the Heart of the Museum? What's Special about Eliyahu's Pita Bread? What is Buddha Doing in a Suburbian House? Who Plays Bowls in the Middle of the Forest? Where Are the Indian Soldiers of His Majesty's Army Buried? What Lurks Near the Entrance to Hell? The Cistern that Became a Hamam, and the Hospital that Became a Hotel. How Much Honor Can the High Commissioner Bestow on the Cat? Who Warmed Themselves by the High Commissioner's Hearth? Is the Gate Crooked or Did the Floor Move? Who Built a White Bench by the Mar Elias Monastery? How Did the Concrete of the Gilo Security Wall become Transparent? Where Did the Animals Go When They Left Noah's Ark? Where Do the Stairs from the Mall Parking Lot Lead? A Work of Art Made to be Walked On. Where is the Brother of the Sundial on Jaffa Road? What Happens at Mahaneh Yehudah Market After the Vegetable Stall Owners Close for the Day? Where is the Entrance to the World's Most Secret Kabbalah Center? Where Did the Greek Patriarch, St. Simon, and Saul Tchernichowski Meet? How Far Were the Limbs of Og, the King of Bashan, Scattered? Where Can You Find Mohammad's Trusty Friend? The Secrets of the Armenian Garden of Eden. After Whom is Jimmy's Alley in the German Colony Named? Who Taught Sir Moses Montefiore to Build the Flour Mill? Who Dared Replace Jerusalem Stone With Tin Plating? The Oldest Villa in Rehavia. Where Are Prayers Translated into Paintings? The Synagogue Over the Catholic Chapel. What Happens When the Rabbi Dies in the Middle of the War? Who Lives Inside the Israel Museum?

The Artist's Bench Who Painted the Holy Land

Imagine the cultural riches of new Jerusalem, the western part of the city as it began to evolve towards the end of the nineteenth century. Consulates from countries around the world appeared there, and the foreign consuls brought with them the customs of their far-off lands. The Emperor and Empress of Ethiopia lived here. Baron de Rothschild built entire neighborhoods and Eliezer Ben-Yehuda revived the Hebrew language as he strolled along the city's streets. All manner of artists came to Jerusalem, including Conrad Schick (who designed the Meah She'arim ultra-orthodox district), poetess Rachel, who came to Jerusalem to benefit from its dry climate and recover from tuberculosis, and British painter William Holman Hunt, one of Britain's most important artists, who built a house in Jerusalem and began to paint biblical motifs.

In England, Holman Hunt (1827–1910) founded an important artistic movement called the Pre-Raphaelite Brotherhood, and acted as its head. The movement emerged during the reign of Queen Victoria. That was a time of political stability, and this is also reflected in the art from that period. There was a wide consensus in the arts in Victorian Britain as Queen Victoria defined and determined artistic tastes, and the royal family and aristocracy followed her lead.

The national Victorian approach reflected an appreciation of the medieval style, in other words, a traditional-religious approach. These artistic tendencies were highlighted by the founding of the Pre-Raphaelite Brotherhood by Holman Hunt. This was a pact made by seven young artists in 1848, including painter and poet Dante Gabriel Rossetti, according to which their works were to express, simply and faithfully, sincere and serious concepts based on direct observation of nature. The artistic authority to which they adhered was the works that preceded Italian painter Raphael, known primarily from etchings.

The amazing innovation in their work was the quality of the colors, which were shiny and bright, and whose intensity was enhanced by the use of pure white as a foundation. For the modern-day observer, the brightness and clarity of pre-Raphaelite works comprises a considerable advantage in Victorian art. This is not

the case with the moralistic content that typifies these works. In the *Awakening Conscience*, for example, which Holman Hunt painted in 1854, one sees a young "frivolous" woman suddenly rising from her lover's lap as her conscience awakens, and she can be seen to be achieving an exalted state of spirituality.

The pre-Raphaelite movement did not last long and most of the members integrated into other artistic styles. Holman Hunt, however, adhered to the style he founded and, to this end, moved far away from his London residence to Jerusalem in search of biblical subjects for his works.

He built his house on ha-Nevi'im Street in Jerusalem in 1869, spent most of his time with leaders of the city's Jewish community, and painted subjects from the Bible against authentic landscapes. In his famous painting *The Finding of the Savior in the Temple*, Holman Hunt portrayed the 12-year-old Jesus arguing with the Jewish sages in the Temple. In order to imbue his work with authenticity and truth, the painter looked for models in the Jewish community of Jerusalem. However, he soon found himself ostracized by the Jews for fear their image may be displayed in a church. Holman Hunt's explanations of the importance of art were to no avail, and he was forced to complete the painting in London with the help of converted Jews.

After his death in 1910, Holman Hunt's wife placed a large majestic stone bench on a hill overlooking the wonderful landscape where her husband used to position his easel while he painted. The stone bears inscriptions in his memory in three languages – English, Arabic, and Hebrew. The hill and the bench are located by the road that leads to the district of Gilo, at the foot of the Mar Elias (the saint Elijah) Monastery, which is familiar to all passers-by.

Despite the position of the bench, and despite its size and the gleam of the white stone, no one notices it. Due to its location by the side of a major road, it is hardly likely that the drivers, rushing past at high speed, notice it and ponder its story, which is also the story of Jerusalem's glorious past.

The Mar Elias Monastery, on Derekh Hevron [Hebron Way], at the entrance to the district of Gilo.

Who Founded an African Village on the Roof of the Church of the Holy Sepulcher? What Do the Nuns Do at the Sixth Station? Is this a Synagogue or a Church? What Can You Find on the Second Floor of the Drapery Store? What's on Offer at Antioch's Descendants' Museum? Who is Really Buried in the Architects' Grave at Jaffa Gate? Where Can You Find a Neighborhood Oven to Use? What's on the Bridge Over the Way to the Western Wall? How to Get to Vienna Via the Old City? Why is the English Princess Buried in a Russian Church? The House Above the Floor of the Armenian Church. Where Did President Ben-Zvi Find a Quiet Spot? With Whom Did Richard Gere Share the "Fourth Wife's Room"? What Lies Shimmering at the Heart of the Museum? What's Special about Eliyahu's Pita Bread? What is Buddha Doing in a Suburbian House? Who Plays Bowls in the Middle of the Forest? Where Are the Indian Soldiers of His Majesty's Army Buried? What Lurks Near the Entrance to Hell? The Cistern that Became a Hamam, and the Hospital that Became a Hotel. How Much Honor Can the High Commissioner Bestow on the Cat? Who Warmed Themselves by the High Commissioner's Hearth? Is the Gate Crooked or Did the Floor Move? Who Built a White Bench by the Mar Elias Monastery? **How Did the Concrete of the Gilo Security Wall become Transparent?** Where Did the Animals Go When They Left Noah's Ark? Where Do the Stairs from the Mall Parking Lot Lead? A Work of Art Made to be Walked On. Where is the Brother of the Sundial on Jaffa Road? What Happens at Mahaneh Yehudah Market After the Vegetable Stall Owners Close for the Day? Where is the Entrance to the World's Most Secret Kabbalah Center? Where Did the Greek Patriarch, St. Simon, and Saul Tchernichowski Meet? How Far Were the Limbs of Og, the King of Bashan, Scattered? Where Can You Find Mohammad's Trusty Friend? The Secrets of the Armenian Garden of Eden. After Whom is Jimmy's Alley in the German Colony Named? Who Taught Sir Moses Montefiore to Build the Flour Mill? Who Dared Replace Jerusalem Stone With Tin Plating? The Oldest Villa in Rehavia. Where Are Prayers Translated into Paintings? The Synagogue Over the Catholic Chapel. What Happens When the Rabbi Dies in the Middle of the War? Who Lives Inside the Israel Museum?

The Transparent Concrete

One day in the middle of Sukkot (Tabernacles, a Jewish holiday) in 2000, shooting began on the district of Gilo, coming from the village of Beit Jallah on the other side of the valley. The situation was so unreal that Gilo residents were initially confused and amazed. It was only later that they began to feel afraid.

Beit Jallah is a small, picturesque village close to Gilo's southern buildings. The villagers were accustomed to cross the valley on foot to get to Jerusalem to shop or run other errands at the shopping center.

Gilo, on the other hand, is a large district with, for example, twice the number of inhabitants as the southern resort of Eilat, with a population in excess of 40,000. It is a quiet district or, as such areas are sometimes known, a bedroom commuity. There are large stone buildings alongside streets with private houses, parks, wide streets – possibly too wide – to be found in the newer districts, used more by cars than by pedestrians.

This is not one of the older romantic Jerusalem districts which sprang up as soon as the first people started branching out from the Old City. This is an area that started immediately after the Six-Day War as part of the security belt constructed around Jerusalem. The security belt is composed of the districts of Ramot, Pisgat Ze'ev, and Neveh Yaakov to the north, and East Talpiyyot to the east. Gilo sprang up on the south, near Bethlehem, named after the biblical settlement of Gilo where Ahitophel the Gilonite, the advisor of King David's son Absalom, lived.

Life in such a large district like Gilo has its own dynamics. Despite the fact that it is connected to Jerusalem, and most of the residents work in the center of the city, its size generates a lively community life. There are numerous schools there, shopping centers, and a community administration, which is like a scaled-down municipality, that takes care of the district's affairs. This is a district with a young and new spirit, described by one of its planners, architect Saul Hirschman as follows: "I dreamt of a border house in the shape of a residential district, with an inside and an outside and a wall. I opened gates at all its corners. I wanted people returning home to first open the gate to the

district. In the heart of the district, I saw a green square, a sort of residential yard for the houses around it. I wanted the gates to be like large windows overlooking olive trees. I wanted people who passed through the district to gain a special experience!"

Although life in a new, large district that overlooks great expanses and open landscapes offers a different experience from life in an old, crowded and closed in neighborhood, the most outstanding experience is that of the residents of the southern end of the area. The streets here lie opposite the spectacular view of Bethlehem and Beit Jallah. From the windows of the buildings here the residents can see the Cremisan Monastery, olive trees and the holy landscapes of Bethlehem.

The residents of these streets were always considered lucky. The entire world yearns for the holy sites while the residents of ha-Anafa Street see them everyday, all day. That was until that evening in September 2000 when a barrage of gunfire was unleashed on the houses there, and pieces of Jerusalem stone began flying in all directions.

For months, life in the neighborhood was frenzied. Many people made the "pilgrimage" to ha-Anafa Street to see how the quiet suburban street had become a battlefield; mobile broadcasting units and reporters from all over the world took up station there by the entrances to the buildings, and the prime minister and his ministers made regular visits there.

Gradually, the local residents learned how to deal with the situation. The windows facing the beautiful landscape were reinforced and narrowed down to the diameter of a gun barrel, and a massive high concrete wall was built along the length of the street. The wall acted as a buffer between the neighborhoods but also obscured the beautiful view. There were no more olive trees and green expanses to look out onto, just an ugly grey wall to which the residents owed their lives.

In fact, just when the guns roared in Gilo, the muses provided Jerusalem's artists with inspiration, and they came up with a wonderful idea. They would adorn the wall with exactly the same view the residents had become used to seeing every day. Around 20 Jerusalem artists set to the task, and spent long hours painting trees, flowers, houses, and churches on the security wall.

The result is so accurate that, initially, it is hard to differentiate between the painting and the real thing. It is only when you become used to it that you realize that you are, in fact, looking at an enormous work of art that stretches along the entire length of Jerusalem's southernmost streets.

Ha-Anafa Street, Gilo.

Who Founded an African Village on the Roof of the Church of the Holy Sepulcher? What Do the Nuns Do at the Sixth Station? Is this a Synagogue or a Church? What Can You Find on the Second Floor of the Drapery Store? What's on Offer at Antioch's Descendants' Museum? Who is Really Buried in the Architects' Grave at Jaffa Gate? Where Can You Find a Neighborhood Oven to Use? What's on the Bridge Over the Way to the Western Wall? How to Get to Vienna Via the Old City? Why is the English Princess Buried in a Russian Church? The House Above the Floor of the Armenian Church. Where Did President Ben-Zvi Find a Quiet Spot? With Whom Did Richard Gere Share the "Fourth Wife's Room"? What Lies Shimmering at the Heart of the Museum? What's Special about Eliyahu's Pita Bread? What is Buddha Doing in a Suburbian House? Who Plays Bowls in the Middle of the Forest? Where Are the Indian Soldiers of His Majesty's Army Buried? What Lurks Near the Entrance to Hell? The Cistern that Became a Hamam, and the Hospital that Became a Hotel. How Much Honor Can the High Commissioner Bestow on the Cat? Who Warmed Themselves by the High Commissioner's Hearth? Is the Gate Crooked or Did the Floor Move? Who Built a White Bench by the Mar Elias Monastery? How Did the Concrete of the Gilo Security Wall become Transparent? Where Did the Animals Go When They Left Noah's Ark? Where Do the Stairs from the Mall Parking Lot Lead? A Work of Art Made to be Walked On. Where is the Brother of the Sundial on Jaffa Road? What Happens at Mahaneh Yehudah Market After the Vegetable Stall Owners Close for the Day? Where is the Entrance to the World's Most Secret Kabbalah Center? Where Did the Greek Patriarch, St. Simon, and Saul Tchernichowski Meet? How Far Were the Limbs of Og, the King of Bashan, Scattered? Where Can You Find Mohammad's Trusty Friend? The Secrets of the Armenian Garden of Eden. After Whom is Jimmy's Alley in the German Colony Named? Who Taught Sir Moses Montefiore to Build the Flour Mill? Who Dared Replace Jerusalem Stone With Tin Plating? The Oldest Villa in Rehavia. Where Are Prayers Translated into Paintings? The Synagogue Over the Catholic Chapel. What Happens When the Rabbi Dies in the Middle of the War? Who Lives Inside the Israel Museum?

Two by Two, They Climbed onto the Hill in the Biblical Zoo

Teddy Kollek, Jerusalem's legendary mayor, had a dream – to sculpt a modern day Noah's Ark in the city where different animals would live. The biblical story gave him a sense of hope for the future, a future in which different communities would live side by side, in harmony, in Jerusalem. In his mind's eye Kollek saw Jerusalem as a center of eternal tolerance, hope, and the ability to survive.

He began to realize his dream in 1971, when he met the French sculptress Nicki de St. Paul who came to Jerusalem to give the city a sculpture which Jerusalemites call The Monster, although de St. Paul created it as The Golem. The name refers to the Golem of Prague, the mystical figure of the Rabbi Judah Loew ben Bezalel, the Maharal of Prague, and de St. Paul believed the Golem's place was in Jerusalem.

The sculpture – a giant imaginary figure with bulging eyes and mouth from which three tongues protrude and with wild spikes bulging from its body – gives the sense of a legendary creation, somewhere between an amiable senseless creature and a frightening monster. It is located in the Kiryat ha-Yovel neighborhood, on the main road leading to Hadassah Hospital.

It seems that from the moment Kollek met the French artist and got to know her work, he decided that she would build Noah's Ark in Jerusalem for him. Kollek's close friends, who knew of his dream, got together to make it come true. Thirty years later, on Kollek's 90th birthday, they dedicated Noah's Ark at a festive ceremony, to Jerusalem. Nicki de St. Paul died soon after this so Noah's Ark is considered her last work.

The work incorporates giant animal figures sculpted by de St. Paul, and an impressive stone ark built by the artist Mario Botte, and stands on the top of a hill at the Biblical Zoo in Malha.

Large sculptures of 23 colorful animals, made of pieces of colorful pottery, shards of glass, and mirror splinters (probably inspired by Antonio Gaudi), are gathered together, gleaming in the bright sunshine. There you can see a spider, gorilla, giraffe, seal, bear, camel, ostrich, turtles, unicorn, bi-horns, kangaroo, cat, horses, rhinoceros, stag, mythical bird, lion and lioness, ambling elephant, and, of course, a dove. The animals are designed to allow children to climb up them, and inside them, and slide out of them.

Despite its size and color, not many people visit the work or even know of its existence. This may be because it is composed of two parts – the animals that have already left the ark, and the ark itself which only contains the heavy elephant which hasn't found the way out yet to join the others. The many visitors to the zoo pass by the two parts of the work, enchanted by the birds in the pond, and ignore this special sculpture which surrounds them. All they have to do to see the colorful animals is to climb up the hill – a small effort for such a special work of art.

The Biblical Zoo, Malha.

Who Founded an African Village on the Roof of the Church of the Holy Sepulcher? What Do the Nuns Do at the Sixth Station? Is this a Synagogue or a Church? What Can You Find on the Second Floor of the Drapery Store? What's on Offer at Antioch's Descendants' Museum? Who is Really Buried in the Architects' Grave at Jaffa Gate? Where Can You Find a Neighborhood Oven to Use? What's on the Bridge Over the Way to the Western Wall? How to Get to Vienna Via the Old City? Why is the English Princess Buried in a Russian Church? The House Above the Floor of the Armenian Church. Where Did President Ben-Zvi Find a Quiet Spot? With Whom Did Richard Gere Share the "Fourth Wife's Room"? What Lies Shimmering at the Heart of the Museum? What's Special about Eliyahu's Pita Bread? What is Buddha Doing in a Suburbian House? Who Plays Bowls in the Middle of the Forest? Where Are the Indian Soldiers of His Majesty's Army Buried? What Lurks Near the Entrance to Hell? The Cistern that Became a Hamam, and the Hospital that Became a Hotel. How Much Honor Can the High Commissioner Bestow on the Cat? Who Warmed Themselves by the High Commissioner's Hearth? Is the Gate Crooked or Did the Floor Move? Who Built a White Bench by the Mar Elias Monastery? How Did the Concrete of the Gilo Security Wall become Transparent? Where Did the Animals Go When They Left Noah's Ark? Where Do the Stairs from the Mall Parking Lot Lead? A Work of Art Made to be Walked On. Where is the Brother of the Sundial on Jaffa Road? What Happens at Mahaneh Yehudah Market After the Vegetable Stall Owners Close for the Day? Where is the Entrance to the World's Most Secret Kabbalah Center? Where Did the Greek Patriarch, St. Simon, and Saul Tchernichowski Meet? How Far Were the Limbs of Og, the King of Bashan, Scattered? Where Can You Find Mohammad's Trusty Friend? The Secrets of the Armenian Garden of Eden. After Whom is Jimmy's Alley in the German Colony Named? Who Taught Sir Moses Montefiore to Build the Flour Mill? Who Dared Replace Jerusalem Stone With Tin Plating? The Oldest Villa in Rehavia. Where Are Prayers Translated into Paintings? The Synagogue Over the Catholic Chapel. What Happens When the Rabbi Dies in the Middle of the War? Who Lives Inside the Israel Museum?

A 4,000-Year-Old Canaanite Village
Opposite the Malha Mall

In the upper parking lot at the Malha Mall, opposite Narkiss (Narcissus) Gate, just above the height of the parking lot, is a surprising archeological site. This is an ancient village whose inhabitants were traders – a sort of early shopping mall.

It is surprising to discover that none of the thousands of visitors to the mall ever climb up the wide stone steps leading to the archeological site, and why the steps criss-cross the small hill there.

It seems the stones are remnants of a village that was built here around 4,000 years ago, during the Bronze Age. A typical house survives from the village, with a set of rooms surrounding a courtyard where cooking and baking utensils were found. A pit was discovered in the center, with a ewe buried nearby. Next to the house a public building was found that was probably used to perform ritual ceremonies, as two cult gravestones and a bench for placing sacrificial offerings were discovered in the western section of the building.

In 1985, when work on the mall began, archeologists embarked on a survey of the site and, primarily found tidy piles of stones. The piles of stones apparently were the result of clearing work in order to create a space for farming activities. The piles contained small and large stones, and pottery shards dating from the First Temple period. After the stones had been removed, the archeologist started to find remains of stone walls. After several months of excavations the houses of the village came to light, indicating that a process of creating permanent settlements began 4,000 years ago. The houses, it seems, were built with bricks on foundations of stone. As the village was almost completely destroyed, however, it was not possible to reconstruct it.

According to the finds at the site, the villagers grew crops and reared animals such as sheep, goats, cows, and pigs for their day-to-day needs.

They were also craftsmen, and made pottery and wove fabrics. They sold their wares for metal utensils. Another village was built on the spot two hundred years later. Instead of the brick and clay houses, the second village was based on a regulated plan. Its houses were not huddled together, like its predecessor, but were spacious residences built around a yard.

The houses, as can be seen from the ruins, were made of large blocks of stones in dry brick walls. The interior of the walls was covered in resistant plaster, some of which survives to this day.

The finds in the rooms and yards included pottery, stone vessels, and a few metal utensils, indicating the socio-economic standing of the second village. For example, animal bones were found in the courtyards, mainly of sheep and goats, with some bones belonging to cows, asses, and numerous domesticated pigs. The acorns found there indicate the existence of oak trees in the region. The village economy was based on cattle and dairy products, wool, pig meat for eating and pigskin used for handiwork and clothing. Plant remains found there include wheat, barley, and various types of legumes.

Numerous stone vessels were found in the rooms and yards, such as large grinding utensils and stone hammers that were used to prepare cooking pots and flint vessels and, possibly, also for metalworking. Smaller utensils were also found, such as files for smoothing wood. The discovery of dozens of bronze needles indicates another aspect of the inhabitants' occupations: leather production. Some of the needles are identical to those used by modern-day shoemakers. One of the needles had an eight-centimeter- [3-inch-] long eye affixed to a bone handle, and was similar to a tool used today to make rugs, and wicker baskets, which indicates that the local in habitants worked in weaving and basketwork. The clay vessels found there also attest to the villagers' activities. Pitchers, cooking pots and easily portable vessels could indicate the sale of agricultural produce in the region. It can be said that in the Malha district of 4,000 years ago, as today, there was trading of leather, rugs, baskets, and food products.

It is difficult to estimate the number of inhabitants of the Canaanite Minhat (Malha). It is likely that there were no more than a hundred families who lived there for two or three generations before abandoning the village.

The reasons for leaving the location are also unclear. It seems that the place remained uninhabited until the first centuries of the Common Era, until a fenced-off farm with agricultural terraces was established there. Construction of the terraces required the felling of oak trees which grew throughout the area, and the stones from the Canaanite village were incorporated in the later houses.

Thus, the Malha Mall marks a resumption of life in the region which was a bustling spot as far back as the Canaanite era, as can be seen on the well-tended verdant archeological site in the mall parking lot.

The upper parking lot, Malha Mall.

Who Founded an African Village on the Roof of the Church of the Holy Sepulcher? What Do the Nuns Do at the Sixth Station? Is this a Synagogue or a Church? What Can You Find on the Second Floor of the Drapery Store? What's on Offer at Antioch's Descendants' Museum? Who is Really Buried in the Architects' Grave at Jaffa Gate? Where Can You Find a Neighborhood Oven to Use? What's on the Bridge Over the Way to the Western Wall? How to Get to Vienna Via the Old City? Why is the English Princess Buried in a Russian Church? The House Above the Floor of the Armenian Church. Where Did President Ben-Zvi Find a Quiet Spot? With Whom Did Richard Gere Share the "Fourth Wife's Room"? What Lies Shimmering at the Heart of the Museum? What's Special about Eliyahu's Pita Bread? What is Buddha Doing in a Suburbian House? Who Plays Bowls in the Middle of the Forest? Where Are the Indian Soldiers of His Majesty's Army Buried? What Lurks Near the Entrance to Hell? The Cistern that Became a Hamam, and the Hospital that Became a Hotel. How Much Honor Can the High Commissioner Bestow on the Cat? Who Warmed Themselves by the High Commissioner's Hearth? Is the Gate Crooked or Did the Floor Move? Who Built a White Bench by the Mar Elias Monastery? How Did the Concrete of the Gilo Security Wall become Transparent? Where Did the Animals Go When They Left Noah's Ark? Where Do the Stairs from the Mall Parking Lot Lead? **A Work of Art Made to be Walked On.** Where is the Brother of the Sundial on Jaffa Road? What Happens at Mahaneh Yehudah Market After the Vegetable Stall Owners Close for the Day? Where is the Entrance to the World's Most Secret Kabbalah Center? Where Did the Greek Patriarch, St. Simon, and Saul Tchernichowski Meet? How Far Were the Limbs of Og, the King of Bashan, Scattered? Where Can You Find Mohammad's Trusty Friend? The Secrets of the Armenian Garden of Eden. After Whom is Jimmy's Alley in the German Colony Named? Who Taught Sir Moses Montefiore to Build the Flour Mill? Who Dared Replace Jerusalem Stone With Tin Plating? The Oldest Villa in Rehavia. Where Are Prayers Translated into Paintings? The Synagogue Over the Catholic Chapel. What Happens When the Rabbi Dies in the Middle of the War? Who Lives Inside the Israel Museum?

The Lowest Sculpture in the World in Zion Square

Zion Square is the hub of life in west Jerusalem. The square is home to stores, restaurants, and some of the largest offices in the city. It is also a traffic nodal point. The square is named after Jerusalem's first cinema that operated on the spot. Today, a high rise with stores and offices stands on the site of the cinema.

The square does not attract tourists or strollers. People rush through and by it on their way to work or shopping. It is here, of all places, and not right in the middle of the square, where you can find the world's lowest sculpture.

You don't see it by accident. It doesn't protrude above ground level, and it is the same color as the paving stones around it. In order to get a good look at it, you have to get down on all fours, move slowly towards the pay phones there, ignore the expressions of wonder on the faces of the passers-by, and take a good look at the sculpture.

The sculpture, in fact, is an iron sewer cover, albeit smaller than the standard sewer lids near it but identical to them in material and color. This lid is a work of art, made by Israeli artist Micha Ullman, called *Water*.

The work was placed here by the artist in 1997 and comprises only one half of the work. The other half, which is identical, is located on Frères Street in the Old City, near the New Gate. The work in Zion Square has a sculpted right hand on it (referring to the Scriptures: "If I forget thee Jerusalem, let my right hand forget its cunning"), while the lid in the Old City has a left hand on it. As the lids are identical in size, they can be switched around.

The sculptures were not put there just for beauty's sake, but are an integral part of the Jerusalem subterranean water supply system. Ullman relates how he was surprised to discover that both sections of Jerusalem use the same water system. Despite the above-ground conflict between the two halves of the city, below ground everything is organized and smooth running. There are no conflicts or wars. The water flows as part of a single system that maintains life.

Half of *Water*, on Frères Street, with the
imprint of a left hand.

The work of art deals with water, just as the hand that turns on a tap provides life, and with cooperation and its importance to life in our part of the world. The two hands can work together to achieve progress, or work against each other. They can join together in a handshake, symbolizing peace, or make themselves into two boxing fists. For now, the two hands are in conflict with each other but, because they are part of the same body, will ultimately have to work together.

Micha Ullman describes himself as "a digger." Since the 1970s, he has worked with the land and things beneath the surface. He builds his sculptures so that the observer either stands on or walks over his works, as he believes that makes them an integral part of the sculpture.

People connect with his works through their bodies, physically, and not just by observing them from afar. There is, seemingly, a boundary between what is above ground and what lies below it, and the observer standing on this line, willingly or not, becomes a part of the work.

Ullman's art is the art of relinquishing – foregoing description and explanations. His approach is one of limitation and abstraction. He is considered a post-minimalist artist who attaches great importance to the inclusion of Jewish aspects in his work. All this is reflected in his halved work in Jerusalem.

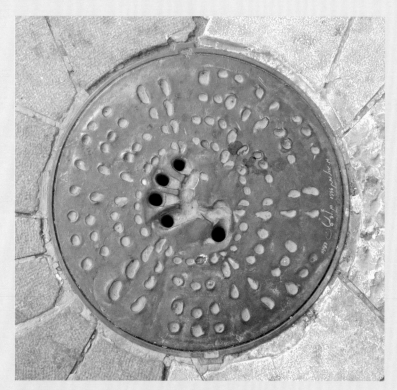

The other half of *Water*, in Zion Square, with the imprint of a right hand.

Zion Square, City center.
Frères St., Christian Quarter, Old City.

140

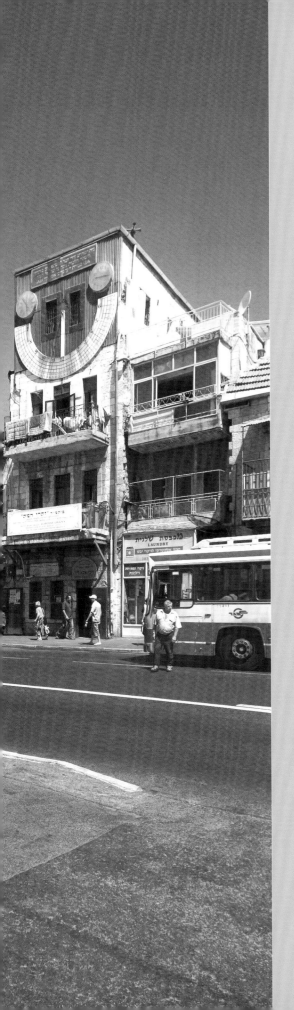

Who Founded an African Village on the Roof of the Church of the Holy Sepulcher? What Do the Nuns Do at the Sixth Station? Is this a Synagogue or a Church? What Can You Find on the Second Floor of the Drapery Store? What's on Offer at Antioch's Descendants' Museum? Who is Really Buried in the Architects' Grave at Jaffa Gate? Where Can You Find a Neighborhood Oven to Use? What's on the Bridge Over the Way to the Western Wall? How to Get to Vienna Via the Old City? Why is the English Princess Buried in a Russian Church? The House Above the Floor of the Armenian Church. Where Did President Ben-Zvi Find a Quiet Spot? With Whom Did Richard Gere Share the "Fourth Wife's Room"? What Lies Shimmering at the Heart of the Museum? What's Special about Eliyahu's Pita Bread? What is Buddha Doing in a Suburbian House? Who Plays Bowls in the Middle of the Forest? Where Are the Indian Soldiers of His Majesty's Army Buried? What Lurks Near the Entrance to Hell? The Cistern that Became a Hamam, and the Hospital that Became a Hotel. How Much Honor Can the High Commissioner Bestow on the Cat? Who Warmed Themselves by the High Commissioner's Hearth? Is the Gate Crooked or Did the Floor Move? Who Built a White Bench by the Mar Elias Monastery? How Did the Concrete of the Gilo Security Wall become Transparent? Where Did the Animals Go When They Left Noah's Ark? Where Do the Stairs from the Mall Parking Lot Lead? A Work of Art Made to be Walked On. Where is the Brother of the Sundial on Jaffa Road? What Happens at Mahaneh Yehudah Market After the Vegetable Stall Owners Close for the Day? Where is the Entrance to the World's Most Secret Kabbalah Center? Where Did the Greek Patriarch, St. Simon, and Saul Tchernichowski Meet? How Far Were the Limbs of Og, the King of Bashan, Scattered? Where Can You Find Mohammad's Trusty Friend? The Secrets of the Armenian Garden of Eden. After Whom is Jimmy's Alley in the German Colony Named? Who Taught Sir Moses Montefiore to Build the Flour Mill? Who Dared Replace Jerusalem Stone With Tin Plating? The Oldest Villa in Rehavia. Where Are Prayers Translated into Paintings? The Synagogue Over the Catholic Chapel. What Happens When the Rabbi Dies in the Middle of the War? Who Lives Inside the Israel Museum?

The Unknown Sundial of 'Sha'arei Hessed'

The sundial in the Sha'arei Hessed district, set in the façade of the Gra synagogue on Yeshayahu Bar Zakai Street, is so anonymous and unknown that it is only alluded to in articles and research papers written about its famous big brother – the sundial in the front wall of the Zoharei Hamma (Sunrise) synagogue on Jaffa Road.

Both clocks were built by sundial expert Rabbi Moses Shapira. The Zoharei Hamma clock was built first, and was installed in 1908 over the third floor of the Hospitality House, which was used to accommodate the many Jewish visitors to Jerusalem who could not find other suitable accommodation. A study room and synagogue were also built, for the visitors' convenience, and where they could pray at sunrise – hence the building's name.

The Sha'arei Hessed sundial, it seems, was installed at a later date, as the neighborhood wasn't established until 1909. The district, at the edge of the Rehavia neighborhood, was used to house religious Ashkenazi Jews. The name Sha'arei Hessed (Gates of Kindness) denotes the kindness of the construction company that allowed observant Jews with limited means to set up homes and bring, as the company put it: "the poor of Jerusalem to their allotted haven so that they need not wander and roam each year from house to house and from place to place."

Rabbi Moses Shapira was assisted by Rabbi Nathanel Sofer, who specialized in the mathematical calculations needed to build the clock, and it was set to Jerusalem time, and not to Cairo time as was the practice in those days. When a sun clock was built on the Temple Mount, in the arches over the wide stairs leading from the Al-Aqsa Mosque to the Dome of the Rock mosque, the Moslem workmen asked Rabbi Moses Shapira to build such a clock on the Temple Mount. They offered him a large sum of money, but Rabbi Shapira refused as Jews are prohibited from entering the Temple Mount.

Thus there are only two sundials made by the artist in Jerusalem (another clock adorns the front of the great Synagogue in Petah Tikva), one popular and familiar, and one hidden away in the district of Sha'arei Hessed.

The Gra synagogue on Yeshayahu Bar Zakai Street, Sha'arei Hessed.

Who Founded an African Village on the Roof of the Church of the Holy Sepulcher? What Do the Nuns Do at the Sixth Station? Is this a Synagogue or a Church? What Can You Find on the Second Floor of the Drapery Store? What's on Offer at Antioch's Descendants' Museum? Who is Really Buried in the Architects' Grave at Jaffa Gate? Where Can You Find a Neighborhood Oven to Use? What's on the Bridge Over the Way to the Western Wall? How to Get to Vienna Via the Old City? Why is the English Princess Buried in a Russian Church? The House Above the Floor of the Armenian Church. Where Did President Ben-Zvi Find a Quiet Spot? With Whom Did Richard Gere Share the "Fourth Wife's Room"? What Lies Shimmering at the Heart of the Museum? What's Special about Eliyahu's Pita Bread? What is Buddha Doing in a Suburbian House? Who Plays Bowls in the Middle of the Forest? Where Are the Indian Soldiers of His Majesty's Army Buried? What Lurks Near the Entrance to Hell? The Cistern that Became a Hamam, and the Hospital that Became a Hotel. How Much Honor Can the High Commissioner Bestow on the Cat? Who Warmed Themselves by the High Commissioner's Hearth? Is the Gate Crooked or Did the Floor Move? Who Built a White Bench by the Mar Elias Monastery? How Did the Concrete of the Gilo Security Wall become Transparent? Where Did the Animals Go When They Left Noah's Ark? Where Do the Stairs from the Mall Parking Lot Lead? A Work of Art Made to be Walked On. Where is the Brother of the Sundial on Jaffa Road? What Happens at Mahaneh Yehudah Market After the Vegetable Stall Owners Close for the Day? Where is the Entrance to the World's Most Secret Kabbalah Center? Where Did the Greek Patriarch, St. Simon, and Saul Tchernichowski Meet? How Far Were the Limbs of Og, the King of Bashan, Scattered? Where Can You Find Mohammad's Trusty Friend? The Secrets of the Armenian Garden of Eden. After Whom is Jimmy's Alley in the German Colony Named? Who Taught Sir Moses Montefiore to Build the Flour Mill? Who Dared Replace Jerusalem Stone With Tin Plating? The Oldest Villa in Rehavia. Where Are Prayers Translated into Paintings? The Synagogue Over the Catholic Chapel. What Happens When the Rabbi Dies in the Middle of the War? Who Lives Inside the Israel Museum?

The Pleasure Seekers Open for Business in the Market

Mahaneh Yehudah is the largest of Jerusalem's markets, and the most exciting. The crowded market, with its enticing scents, is a feast for the senses. This is undoubtedly a place imbued with the very essence of Jerusalem authenticity. If you want to eat well, and grab a tasty humus, the market is the place to go. If you want to analyze Saturday's soccer match, you go to the stall owners, and if you want to join the hierarchy of a political party – any political party – you do the rounds of the market.

The market was established during the Ottoman Era and was originally called the Beit Yaakov (House of Jacob) Market. Arab traders from the area would go there to sell their produce. At this time, the market grew and spread out in a disorganized fashion. The sanitation conditions deteriorated to the point that, in the 1920s, the British administration ordered the traders to evacuate the spot and to shut the health hazard down.

As the city was now left without a market, the Urban Committee for the Jews of Jerusalem entered the picture under the leadership of Samuel Meir Mussaief, who was also the head of the Loan and Savings Bank. The committee gathered the Jewish traders together and arranged for them to receive easy loans from the bank so that they could build an orderly market. The bank agreed to provide the loans on condition that the market was named after it.

Construction of the new market was completed in 1931, and a sign with the market's official name – The Loan and Savings Bank – was placed at 2 ha-Shaked Street. The sign is still there. However, this name never stuck and Jerusalemites preferred the name Mahaneh Yehudah, which was the name given to the

adjoining neighborhood that was built in 1887. The person who acquired the land for the district from the Arabs was Joseph Navon, a businessman who had interests in many fields who, among other projects, initiated the construction of the Jerusalem-Jaffa railroad. He named the district after his brother Judah (Yehudah), who died young.

In recent years, the market has undergone renovation and re-roofing work, giving a more modern look and allowing shoppers to buy their food, summer and winter, in market ambiance but in the conditions of a modern shopping mall. The authentic atmosphere of the market is zealously preserved.

Throughout the day, the market looks like a colorful painting while in the evening, the alleyways are deserted. The color disappears and silence replaces the daytime hustle and bustle. Recently, however, Jerusalem night owls have discovered something new there – a whole alley that changes its entire character. The vegetable stalls become all-purpose tables. Diners crowd round the tables/stalls and waiters dash between them carrying plates laden with tasty dishes. Meanwhile, a jazz band which took up position on some the steps of the spice store, and wrapped itself in a thick blue cloud of cigarette smoke, plays delicate tunes.

Light filters into the market from a special café that recently opened up on ha-Sheizaf Street, inside a typical household goods market store called Everything for the Baker and Coffee. The café operates during the market's business hours, and sometimes at night as well, adding a new breath of life to the market. Artists display their work there, and night owls stop by for a cup of coffee and to listen to some music.

The alley has also taken on a new lease of life. Designer clothes stores have opened up, as well as an Israeli winery and a delicatessen. It has to be said, this is without doubt the first yuppie revolution at Mahaneh Yehudah Market.

ha-Sheizaf Street, Mahaneh Yehudah Market.

Who Founded an African Village on the Roof of the Church of the Holy Sepulcher? What Do the Nuns Do at the Sixth Station? Is this a Synagogue or a Church? What Can You Find on the Second Floor of the Drapery Store? What's on Offer at Antioch's Descendants' Museum? Who is Really Buried in the Architects' Grave at Jaffa Gate? Where Can You Find a Neighborhood Oven to Use? What's on the Bridge Over the Way to the Western Wall? How to Get to Vienna Via the Old City? Why is the English Princess Buried in a Russian Church? The House Above the Floor of the Armenian Church. Where Did President Ben-Zvi Find a Quiet Spot? With Whom Did Richard Gere Share the "Fourth Wife's Room"? What Lies Shimmering at the Heart of the Museum? What's Special about Eliyahu's Pita Bread? What is Buddha Doing in a Suburbian House? Who Plays Bowls in the Middle of the Forest? Where Are the Indian Soldiers of His Majesty's Army Buried? What Lurks Near the Entrance to Hell? The Cistern that Became a Hamam, and the Hospital that Became a Hotel. How Much Honor Can the High Commissioner Bestow on the Cat? Who Warmed Themselves by the High Commissioner's Hearth? Is the Gate Crooked or Did the Floor Move? Who Built a White Bench by the Mar Elias Monastery? How Did the Concrete of the Gilo Security Wall become Transparent? Where Did the Animals Go When They Left Noah's Ark? Where Do the Stairs from the Mall Parking Lot Lead? A Work of Art Made to be Walked On. Where is the Brother of the Sundial on Jaffa Road? What Happens at Mahaneh Yehudah Market After the Vegetable Stall Owners Close for the Day? **Where is the Entrance to the World's Most Secret Kabbalah Center?** Where Did the Greek Patriarch, St. Simon, and Saul Tchernichowski Meet? How Far Were the Limbs of Og, the King of Bashan, Scattered? Where Can You Find Mohammad's Trusty Friend? The Secrets of the Armenian Garden of Eden. After Whom is Jimmy's Alley in the German Colony Named? Who Taught Sir Moses Montefiore to Build the Flour Mill? Who Dared Replace Jerusalem Stone With Tin Plating? The Oldest Villa in Rehavia. Where Are Prayers Translated into Paintings? The Synagogue Over the Catholic Chapel. What Happens When the Rabbi Dies in the Middle of the War? Who Lives Inside the Israel Museum?

Messiah, the Son of David and the Olive Trees behind the Edison Cinema

At "the top of the hill," which is called that for a reason, between two olive trees – not just any two olive trees – Jerusalem kabbalists daily await the appearance of Messiah, the son of Joseph, as written in the talmudic tractate of Sanhedrin.

According to the Jewish view of redemption, there are two concepts – Messiah the son of Joseph and Messiah the son of David – parallel to the two stages of the expected redemption. First, Messiah the son of Joseph will appear, bringing with him the tangible redemption. According to the Babylonian Talmud, this Messiah will be killed, and only after that will Messiah the son of David appear, bringing with him the complete redemption of a spiritual-moral nature. Between these two stages, the people of Israel will experience difficult times, known as "the birth pangs of the Messiah."

The term "the top of the hill" is not a geographical description of a specific place. Instead, it is a kabbalistic concept according to which the sanctity of "the top of the hill," on which Moses stood during the war against Amalek transferred to this "top of the hill," on Prague Street, north of Bikur Holim Hospital, in the Ezrat Israel district on noisy Straus Street. The Kabbalists who come here add that the *gematria* (sum of the numerical value of the Hebrew letters) of "the top of the hill" is the equivalent of "Jerusalem" in Hebrew.

The ancient thick-trunked olive trees at the top of the hill stand like old sentries. According to the Kabbalah, this is the entrance to Jerusalem – *"pitha de-karta"* – a gate to an invisible wall, or an imaginary circle that surrounds and guards Jerusalem, and all that can be seen from the spot is the two great olive trees.

Jerusalem's Kabbalists determined that this is the spot where Messiah the son of Joseph will appear, based on the book of Zohar, which says that the Messiah the son of David's place is inside Jerusalem, while the place of Messiah the son of Joseph is outside Jerusalem, i.e., the area known as "the interim line."

Kabbalists have always held ceremonies and prayers there. In the time when all Jews lived within the Old City walls, the heads of the Ashkenazi and Sephardi communities endeavored to redeem the spot that was far away from the center of Jewish life in the Old City. The Kabbalists rented the spot from the Arab landowners on an annual basis. For seventy years between the olive trees at the top of the hill, there was a tent that was called the Tent of Messiah the son of Joseph where Kabbalists studied the Kabbalah and prayed.

In 1888, thirty years after the first Jews left the Old City and the new section of Jerusalem began developing, the site was acquired from its Arab owners for a hefty sum. Immediately after the acquisition, Jews began settling nearby, and the district of Ezrat Israel sprang up.

As the space between the olive trees is believed to have the power to bring victory in battle (for the same powers which were ascribed to the hill upon which Moses stood with his arms raised, thereby helping gain victory over Amalek, have been transferred to this spot), during the siege of Jerusalem in the 1948 War of Independence, Kabbalists set up a giant tent here and held prayer sessions. Participants in the prayer sessions say that as soon as prayers began, there was an improvement in the security situation around Jerusalem and the bombardment abated.

Today, the two olive trees are surrounded by a playground where small children play and hide behind them without knowing anything about the sacred importance of the spot.

Prague Street, between Strauss Street and Yeshayahu Street.

Who Founded an African Village on the Roof of the Church of the Holy Sepulcher? What Do the Nuns Do at the Sixth Station? Is this a Synagogue or a Church? What Can You Find on the Second Floor of the Drapery Store? What's on Offer at Antioch's Descendants' Museum? Who is Really Buried in the Architects' Grave at Jaffa Gate? Where Can You Find a Neighborhood Oven to Use? What's on the Bridge Over the Way to the Western Wall? How to Get to Vienna Via the Old City? Why is the English Princess Buried in a Russian Church? The House Above the Floor of the Armenian Church. Where Did President Ben-Zvi Find a Quiet Spot? With Whom Did Richard Gere Share the "Fourth Wife's Room"? What Lies Shimmering at the Heart of the Museum? What's Special about Eliyahu's Pita Bread? What is Buddha Doing in a Suburbian House? Who Plays Bowls in the Middle of the Forest? Where Are the Indian Soldiers of His Majesty's Army Buried? What Lurks Near the Entrance to Hell? The Cistern that Became a Hamam, and the Hospital that Became a Hotel. How Much Honor Can the High Commissioner Bestow on the Cat? Who Warmed Themselves by the High Commissioner's Hearth? Is the Gate Crooked or Did the Floor Move? Who Built a White Bench by the Mar Elias Monastery? How Did the Concrete of the Gilo Security Wall become Transparent? Where Did the Animals Go When They Left Noah's Ark? Where Do the Stairs from the Mall Parking Lot Lead? A Work of Art Made to be Walked On. Where is the Brother of the Sundial on Jaffa Road? What Happens at Mahaneh Yehudah Market After the Vegetable Stall Owners Close for the Day? Where is the Entrance to the World's Most Secret Kabbalah Center? Where Did the Greek Patriarch, St. Simon, and Saul Tchernichowski Meet? How Far Were the Limbs of Og, the King of Bashan, Scattered? Where Can You Find Mohammad's Trusty Friend? The Secrets of the Armenian Garden of Eden. After Whom is Jimmy's Alley in the German Colony Named? Who Taught Sir Moses Montefiore to Build the Flour Mill? Who Dared Replace Jerusalem Stone With Tin Plating? The Oldest Villa in Rehavia. Where Are Prayers Translated into Paintings? The Synagogue Over the Catholic Chapel. What Happens When the Rabbi Dies in the Middle of the War? Who Lives Inside the Israel Museum?

The Trilateral Meeting at the St. Simon Monastery

In the heart of a well-tended park in the district of Old Katamon is a tiny church that looks like a playground in a green garden. The church's diminutive dimensions look even more striking against the backdrop of tall buildings that surround it. Its miniature size notwithstanding, the building has all the elements of a regular-sized church: a silver dome topped by a cross; a thin delicate-looking turret belonging to a bell tower, and a priest who appears from the building from time to time.

This is the Greek Orthodox St. Simon Monastery that even Jerusalemites who have heard of it have never come across owing to its concealed position. Even fewer know that the nearby district of Katamon takes its name from Katamonis, meaning "near the monastery" in Greek. The monastery is part of a complex that once included the summer house of the Greek patriarch. The summer house now serves as a center for physically disabled people, while the church is cared for by a single priest who lives nearby. The church opens for prayers on Sundays, but few attend. At the end of prayers, the gate is locked and remains shut until the following Sunday.

Over the entrance to the monastery is a plaque which tells of "Abramios, a monk from Aditus, the builder of the holy monastery on the ruins of the holy grave of Katamon of today, and the entire surrounding area, during the time of the Patriarch Cyril the Second in 1859, who for over twenty years, endured great suffering and bore heavy expenses in order to build over these ancient ruins new buildings and a divine church containing the holy grave of St. Simon. He also prepared the area and planted hundreds of olive trees at his own expense and dedicated these buildings to the holy community of the holy grave. He entrusted the keys of this small monastery to His Holiness the Patriarch of Jerusalem, Lerotheos in 1879, to the memory of himself and his parents, February 3 1881."

The ancient ruins over which the monastery was built are of the thirteenth-century Gregorian monastery was completely destroyed in the sixteenth-century. The monastery is generally known as St. Simon, although its real name is Hagios Simonis St. Simon.

St. Simon was a Jew who converted to Christianity and who believed that the infant Jesus was destined to be the Messiah. The New Testament says about him: "And here was a man in Jerusalem, called Simon, a righteous and pious person and awaiting Israel's comfort and the Holy Spirit rests with him and it was revealed to him by the Holy Spirit that he would not die until he had seen the Lord's Messiah, and he will come with the spirit to the Temple, and the fathers brought the child Jesus… and they held him in their arms and God gave a blessing saying… my eyes have seen your salvation… a light unto the nations (Luke 2:25–36).

According to Christian tradition the righteous man lived in the place where the monastery was built and inside the church. His burial place can be seen hewn out of the rock. In the 1930s, poet Saul Tchernichowski lived there, and died there. During the War of Independence, the South Jerusalem Irregular Palestinian Forces command was stationed here. As part of the Yevusi campaign, hard battles were waged here, that exacted a heavy toll on the Palmah's fourth battalion. In April 1948, the monastery was captured along with the nearby Katamon district.

This small place has witnessed many changes. It is no surprise that its history, which is intertwined with that of Jerusalem, is familiar to all of us but, despite this, not many know of the small concealed monastery whose gates are always locked.

St. Simon Monastery, Bnei Beteira Street, Old Katamon.

Who Founded an African Village on the Roof of the Church of the Holy Sepulcher? What Do the Nuns Do at the Sixth Station? Is this a Synagogue or a Church? What Can You Find on the Second Floor of the Drapery Store? What's on Offer at Antioch's Descendants' Museum? Who is Really Buried in the Architects' Grave at Jaffa Gate? Where Can You Find a Neighborhood Oven to Use? What's on the Bridge Over the Way to the Western Wall? How to Get to Vienna Via the Old City? Why is the English Princess Buried in a Russian Church? The House Above the Floor of the Armenian Church. Where Did President Ben-Zvi Find a Quiet Spot? With Whom Did Richard Gere Share the "Fourth Wife's Room"? What Lies Shimmering at the Heart of the Museum? What's Special about Eliyahu's Pita Bread? What is Buddha Doing in a Suburbian House? Who Plays Bowls in the Middle of the Forest? Where Are the Indian Soldiers of His Majesty's Army Buried? What Lurks Near the Entrance to Hell? The Cistern that Became a Hamam, and the Hospital that Became a Hotel. How Much Honor Can the High Commissioner Bestow on the Cat? Who Warmed Themselves by the High Commissioner's Hearth? Is the Gate Crooked or Did the Floor Move? Who Built a White Bench by the Mar Elias Monastery? How Did the Concrete of the Gilo Security Wall become Transparent? Where Did the Animals Go When They Left Noah's Ark? Where Do the Stairs from the Mall Parking Lot Lead? A Work of Art Made to be Walked On. Where is the Brother of the Sundial on Jaffa Road? What Happens at Mahaneh Yehudah Market After the Vegetable Stall Owners Close for the Day? Where is the Entrance to the World's Most Secret Kabbalah Center? Where Did the Greek Patriarch, St. Simon, and Saul Tchernichowski Meet? **How Far Were the Limbs of Og, the King of Bashan, Scattered?** Where Can You Find Mohammad's Trusty Friend? The Secrets of the Armenian Garden of Eden. After Whom is Jimmy's Alley in the German Colony Named? Who Taught Sir Moses Montefiore to Build the Flour Mill? Who Dared Replace Jerusalem Stone With Tin Plating? The Oldest Villa in Rehavia. Where Are Prayers Translated into Paintings? The Synagogue Over the Catholic Chapel. What Happens When the Rabbi Dies in the Middle of the War? Who Lives Inside the Israel Museum?

The Marble Column That Was Rejected at the Entrance to the Temple

The Russian Compound is a sort of alley or square that the downtown traffic problems turn into a giant traffic jam. While the drivers nervously wait for the traffic lights to change from red to green, they cannot avoid catching a glimpse of the beautiful Russian church with its copper domes and golden crosses, or the Israeli Police's jail with police officers entering and leaving it. It is, however, unlikely that anyone notices the long iron railings jutting out in the middle of the compound that protects something unseen.

On the railing, half of which is painted in white and half of which is covered in rust, and that looks like any standard balcony railing, normally lean the parents of prison inmates waiting for visiting hours. The railing also bears untidily placed signs declaring that the place is reserved for police cars only. If you take a close look, however, you will find a surprise. The railings encompass a depression in the ground occupied by a giant marble "finger," half exposed and half still unrevealed. Older local residents will tell you that many years ago, long before the traffic took over, there was a playground for the city's children, who called the statue "the finger of Og, King of Bashan," who was killed by the tribes of Israel.

The column was discovered around 150 years ago, when the Russians prepared the land for construction. The theory is that the area once served as a quarry where construction pillars were hewn. However, due to a crack found in this column during the quarry work, it was left there. According to the theory, the column was designated to be used for King Herod's building in Jerusalem, and may even have been meant for the Temple as its dimensions match the description of pillars used there: "Twenty five cubits, and each was made of a single stone" (Josephus, *The Jewish War* 5:6) A similar quarry operated at that time in the area of Mahaneh Yehuda, where two Roman pillars were discovered.

The finger of Og, King of Bashan, lies in one of the most beautiful spots in Jerusalem, between majestic buildings steeped in long history and romance. The area is called the Russian Compound, as it was acquired by the Russians in 1856. The Jews, who planned

158

to acquire the land from its Arab owners, could not match the enormous sum of money the Russians paid – in excess of one million rubles – a fortune in those days.

After the purchase, the Russians put up the first buildings belonging to Christians outside the Old City walls. The buildings were designed for the use of Russian monks who wanted to live in the Holy Land, and to serve as hostels for the large numbers of pilgrims who visited the holy sites. They called the place "Nova Yerusalma" – New Jerusalem. The Russians built there "a small city" that included the Russian consulate and a hostel for women; during the British Mandate, this building served as a jail for political prisoners and members of underground organizations. Here Etzel organization member Meir Feinstein and Lehi member Moshe Barazani were sentenced to death by hanging. Also built here were a Russian hospital; a library that currently serves the district court; and the Holy Triad Church, with copper domes that were originally painted green, which are reminiscent of the Ascension church in Moscow's Kremlin. There was also a hostel for men, half of which is today incorporated in the Israeli Police jail. The hostel is called Sergei's House, after Prince Sergei the brother of Czar Nicholas. The building has two towers which, despite their splendor, were used as the hostel's toilets (one still serves the

same purpose today). Part of the building houses the offices of the Ministry of Agriculture, the Nature Reserves Authority, and the Nature Protection Society.

In 1964, part of the Russian church's assets in the Russian Compound were bought by the Israeli government for $4.5 million. As the Russian government was interested in divesting itself of religious assets, and the Israeli government did not have sufficient funds to pay the full amount, $3 million of the amount was paid in shipments of oranges to Russia over a long period.

The "orange deal" did not apply to all the buildings in the compound and did not include the Sergei Hostel, which is still hotly disputed by the White Church and Red Church in Russia. Even Prince Phillip, the Queen of England's husband, who is a descendant of Prince Sergei, claims ownership of the building.

Meanwhile, while the whole world rages over this small strip of land which has seen many historical dramas, a majestic unknown marble column lies modestly by the side.

The Russian Compound, 1 Heshin Street.

160

Who Founded an African Village on the Roof of the Church of the Holy Sepulcher? What Do the Nuns Do at the Sixth Station? Is this a Synagogue or a Church? What Can You Find on the Second Floor of the Drapery Store? What's on Offer at Antioch's Descendants' Museum? Who is Really Buried in the Architects' Grave at Jaffa Gate? Where Can You Find a Neighborhood Oven to Use? What's on the Bridge Over the Way to the Western Wall? How to Get to Vienna Via the Old City? Why is the English Princess Buried in a Russian Church? The House Above the Floor of the Armenian Church. Where Did President Ben-Zvi Find a Quiet Spot? With Whom Did Richard Gere Share the "Fourth Wife's Room"? What Lies Shimmering at the Heart of the Museum? What's Special about Eliyahu's Pita Bread? What is Buddha Doing in a Suburbian House? Who Plays Bowls in the Middle of the Forest? Where Are the Indian Soldiers of His Majesty's Army Buried? What Lurks Near the Entrance to Hell? The Cistern that Became a Hamam, and the Hospital that Became a Hotel. How Much Honor Can the High Commissioner Bestow on the Cat? Who Warmed Themselves by the High Commissioner's Hearth? Is the Gate Crooked or Did the Floor Move? Who Built a White Bench by the Mar Elias Monastery? How Did the Concrete of the Gilo Security Wall become Transparent? Where Did the Animals Go When They Left Noah's Ark? Where Do the Stairs from the Mall Parking Lot Lead? A Work of Art Made to be Walked On. Where is the Brother of the Sundial on Jaffa Road? What Happens at Mahaneh Yehudah Market After the Vegetable Stall Owners Close for the Day? Where is the Entrance to the World's Most Secret Kabbalah Center? Where Did the Greek Patriarch, St. Simon, and Saul Tchernichowski Meet? How Far Were the Limbs of Og, the King of Bashan, Scattered? Where Can You Find Mohammad's Trusty Friend? The Secrets of the Armenian Garden of Eden. After Whom is Jimmy's Alley in the German Colony Named? Who Taught Sir Moses Montefiore to Build the Flour Mill? Who Dared Replace Jerusalem Stone With Tin Plating? The Oldest Villa in Rehavia. Where Are Prayers Translated into Paintings? The Synagogue Over the Catholic Chapel. What Happens When the Rabbi Dies in the Middle of the War? Who Lives Inside the Israel Museum?

The Grave of Nebi Ukasha in the Center of the City

In the center of town, between busy Straus Street and Yeshayahu Street that runs parallel to it in the Ezrat Israel neighborhood, there is a beautiful, complete ancient building. The building is made of stone and is capped by dome, and by a slender designed turret. You can't miss it as you pass by. Nevertheless no one stops to ponder it and no one knows what it is.

Apparently, the building that sits today in the middle of a playground opposite the local laundry and an optician's is a holy site of great importance to the Islamic world. This is the grave of Ukasha bin Mihsan, friend to the Prophet Mohammad, and a member of the prophet's close circle of friends called the Sahaba. Ukasha was one of the first supporters of Islam. Many stories are told about this amazing figure, and he is said to have had superhuman powers.

One legend relates that Ukasha's sword broke in the middle of a battle, whereupon Mohammad provided him with a branch that turned into a sword. Because of these tales, and his closeness to Mohammad, Ukasha was mistakenly called a prophet, and the site is called Nebi Ukasha (the Prophet Ukasha) instead of simply Ukasha's Grave.

The tomb building and minaret date back to the Mameluke Period, and even the pretty houses from the early twentieth century near by do nothing to detract from its beauty. All you have to do to appreciate it is to look up to the top of the hill and be impressed by the fact that, in Jerusalem, even the most mundane activities are shrouded by holiness.

Prague Street that joins Strauss Street and Yeshayahu Street.

162

The Kumaria: the Kumar family burial estate adjoining the Grave of
Nebi Ukasha

Who Founded an African Village on the Roof of the Church of the Holy Sepulcher? What Do the Nuns Do at the Sixth Station? Is this a Synagogue or a Church? What Can You Find on the Second Floor of the Drapery Store? What's on Offer at Antioch's Descendants' Museum? Who is Really Buried in the Architects' Grave at Jaffa Gate? Where Can You Find a Neighborhood Oven to Use? What's on the Bridge Over the Way to the Western Wall? How to Get to Vienna Via the Old City? Why is the English Princess Buried in a Russian Church? The House Above the Floor of the Armenian Church. Where Did President Ben-Zvi Find a Quiet Spot? With Whom Did Richard Gere Share the "Fourth Wife's Room"? What Lies Shimmering at the Heart of the Museum? What's Special about Eliyahu's Pita Bread? What is Buddha Doing in a Suburbian House? Who Plays Bowls in the Middle of the Forest? Where Are the Indian Soldiers of His Majesty's Army Buried? What Lurks Near the Entrance to Hell? The Cistern that Became a Hamam, and the Hospital that Became a Hotel. How Much Honor Can the High Commissioner Bestow on the Cat? Who Warmed Themselves by the High Commissioner's Hearth? Is the Gate Crooked or Did the Floor Move? Who Built a White Bench by the Mar Elias Monastery? How Did the Concrete of the Gilo Security Wall become Transparent? Where Did the Animals Go When They Left Noah's Ark? Where Do the Stairs from the Mall Parking Lot Lead? A Work of Art Made to be Walked On. Where is the Brother of the Sundial on Jaffa Road? What Happens at Mahaneh Yehudah Market After the Vegetable Stall Owners Close for the Day? Where is the Entrance to the World's Most Secret Kabbalah Center? Where Did the Greek Patriarch, St. Simon, and Saul Tchernichowski Meet? How Far Were the Limbs of Og, the King of Bashan, Scattered? Where Can You Find Mohammad's Trusty Friend? **The Secrets of the Armenian Garden of Eden.** After Whom is Jimmy's Alley in the German Colony Named? Who Taught Sir Moses Montefiore to Build the Flour Mill? Who Dared Replace Jerusalem Stone With Tin Plating? The Oldest Villa in Rehavia. Where Are Prayers Translated into Paintings? The Synagogue Over the Catholic Chapel. What Happens When the Rabbi Dies in the Middle of the War? Who Lives Inside the Israel Museum?

The Ceramic Tile Mural on Coresh Street

In contrast with the Jerusalem tradition that has emerged in recent years, involving the painting of murals on the sides of buildings that stand at major junctions, Marie Balian's work is hidden away on a side street.

The impressive work, called *The Secrets of the Garden of Eden*, is on the wall of Building 14 on Coresh Street. For a change, this is not a painted mural but one of the largest ceramic works ever seen in Jerusalem, a city that has quite a few Armenian murals. Balian dedicated this work to Jerusalem, where she has worked for the past forty years.

The work measures 4 meters by 6 meters [13 feet by 19.5 feet] and is composed of close to 1,000 ceramic tiles. The process of assembling the work was unique, and includes charcoal sketches on the tiles, painting and designing each tile individually, and then firing the tiles in an oven. At the end of the process, the entire picture has to be reassembled.

The Secrets of the Garden of Eden depicts a cosmic idyllic scene that does not refer to the noisy bustling urban reality around it as do other town center murals. The entire work is composed between two framed images of a palm tree and a cypress tree, with a lemon tree and a pomegranate tree, flowers and other vegetation.

A hazy line divides land and sea along the length of the picture. At the foot of the scene is a pair of peacocks, with open tails, with the tail of a third peacock serving as the centerpiece of the whole work. The sea contains flying fish and ancient sailing boats. The trunk of the palm tree stretches diagonally across from the land, and its top spreads out over the sea. The cypress twists and turns into the sea, and its green color stands out against the blue of the water. According to ancient Christian burial art, the palm tree and cypress have symbolic significances relating to eternity and life.

The artist maintains a dialogue with tradition while producing a lucid work reflecting a perfect naïve world that is, nonetheless, dynamic, feminine, and contemporary. In terms of aesthetics, the picture gleams, absorbing and retransmitting rays of light while symbolically projecting promise, as the work sits between the grey walls of a small Jerusalem side street as a hidden, mysterious Garden of Eden.

Historically one can approach the mural in two contexts. The first is the tradition of wall painting developed in the early twentieth century by Mexican painters Diego Rivera, David Alfaro Siqueiros, and José Clemente Orozco. This tradition was used by the artists as a means of expressing their belief that paintings should serve

the revolution of the masses, so that the latter can see the history and results of the revolution.

This tradition was passed on to many cities around the world, whereby all artists shared the common wish to produce public art to act as milestones in the day-to-day voyage of the city dwellers, and to escort them on their way. The tradition also found its way to Jerusalem and, around ten years ago, a group of artists from Lyons, France, was asked to decorate the city. The colorful paintings that overlook the streets depict scenes from the residents' daily lives. For example, the painting on the main street of the Mahaneh Yehudah market depicts a falafel stand and scenes from the neighborhood.

The second context in which one can view *The Secrets of the Garden of Eden* is the heritage of tiled pictures, which has been practiced in Jerusalem for some ninety years. Marie Balian, who was born in Lyons and lived in Jerusalem, was the daughter-in-law of Neshan Balian, a ceramic artist who was brought to Israel with two other artists – David Ohanessian and Magardish Karkashian – from Kütahya, Turkey in 1919 in order to renovate and reconstruct the tiles of the Dome of the Rock.

The three settled in Jerusalem and continued their work through workshops they established and also created large and well-known murals in the city. Marie Balian became the main painter of the Balian workshop, and her works serve as examples of individualist art created within a context of ancient tradition.

14 Coresh Street, downtown Jerusalem.

Who Founded an African Village on the Roof of the Church of the Holy Sepulcher? What Do the Nuns Do at the Sixth Station? Is this a Synagogue or a Church? What Can You Find on the Second Floor of the Drapery Store? What's on Offer at Antioch's Descendants' Museum? Who is Really Buried in the Architects' Grave at Jaffa Gate? Where Can You Find a Neighborhood Oven to Use? What's on the Bridge Over the Way to the Western Wall? How to Get to Vienna Via the Old City? Why is the English Princess Buried in a Russian Church? The House Above the Floor of the Armenian Church. Where Did President Ben-Zvi Find a Quiet Spot? With Whom Did Richard Gere Share the "Fourth Wife's Room"? What Lies Shimmering at the Heart of the Museum? What's Special about Eliyahu's Pita Bread? What is Buddha Doing in a Suburbian House? Who Plays Bowls in the Middle of the Forest? Where Are the Indian Soldiers of His Majesty's Army Buried? What Lurks Near the Entrance to Hell? The Cistern that Became a Hamam, and the Hospital that Became a Hotel. How Much Honor Can the High Commissioner Bestow on the Cat? Who Warmed Themselves by the High Commissioner's Hearth? Is the Gate Crooked or Did the Floor Move? Who Built a White Bench by the Mar Elias Monastery? How Did the Concrete of the Gilo Security Wall become Transparent? Where Did the Animals Go When They Left Noah's Ark? Where Do the Stairs from the Mall Parking Lot Lead? A Work of Art Made to be Walked On. Where is the Brother of the Sundial on Jaffa Road? What Happens at Mahaneh Yehudah Market After the Vegetable Stall Owners Close for the Day? Where is the Entrance to the World's Most Secret Kabbalah Center? Where Did the Greek Patriarch, St. Simon, and Saul Tchernichowski Meet? How Far Were the Limbs of Og, the King of Bashan, Scattered? Where Can You Find Mohammad's Trusty Friend? The Secrets of the Armenian Garden of Eden. After Whom is Jimmy's Alley in the German Colony Named? Who Taught Sir Moses Montefiore to Build the Flour Mill? Who Dared Replace Jerusalem Stone With Tin Plating? The Oldest Villa in Rehavia. Where Are Prayers Translated into Paintings? The Synagogue Over the Catholic Chapel. What Happens When the Rabbi Dies in the Middle of the War? Who Lives Inside the Israel Museum?

The Dog Honored as a King

Jerusalem's German Colony was founded in 1873 by a Christian organization called the Templar Society. For them the "temple" was not a stone building but a group of people creating a divine structure through their faith and presence in the Holy Land.

The Templars came to Israel looking to establish a pure society with Jerusalem as its center. Besides Jerusalem, the Templars established urban colonies in Haifa and Jaffa and an agricultural colony in Tel Aviv, at Wilhelma (Bnei Atarot), Bethlehem in the Galilee, and Waldheim (Alonei Abba).

The community's activities were halted at the outbreak of World War II. Community members identified with the Nazi regime in Germany, and were expelled by the British, who confiscated their houses.

Despite being built with Jerusalem stone, the houses of the German Colony were designed in a European style – square shaped with simple lines. Most of the houses have two stories and a tiled pointed roof. Jerusalemites like the houses of the Colony and have preserved and nurtured them over the years. While a floor may have been added, or a house reconstructed, efforts have been made to adhere to the original style.

The Templars built a network of paths between the houses. Some of the paths became narrow access roads but most remained narrow paths cramped with thick vegetation that affords the houses a degree of privacy. If you turn off the main road and lose yourself between the paths, you can discover charming houses tucked away between the trees that can only be accessed via narrow alleyways.

One of these alleys is close to busy Emek Refaim Street, which has become Jerusalem's main leisure area. The secret alley is not far from Masaryk Café and, as the entrance is largely obscured by vegetation, it is hard to see where it leads.

Local veterans who know every stone and corner in the area call it Jimmy's Alley. It is rare for alleys, which are hardly substantial enough to join two houses, to be given a name. However, this

one not only has a name, it also has a plaque which reads:
The alley of Jimmy, who wagged his tail and happily walked here between 1988 and 1998.

Jimmy, as the residents relate, was a small dachshund who belonged to one of the residents of the street. Jimmy used to walk around the alleys on his own and would frequent the local cafés as if he lived there. The people in the cafés still miss him. The love he received from his owners, and their loyalty to him, as well as the originality they showed in commemorating him are undoubtedly worthy of appreciation.

Jimmy's Alley, Masaryk Street, the German Colony.

Who Founded an African Village on the Roof of the Church of the Holy Sepulcher? What Do the Nuns Do at the Sixth Station? Is this a Synagogue or a Church? What Can You Find on the Second Floor of the Drapery Store? What's on Offer at Antioch's Descendants' Museum? Who is Really Buried in the Architects' Grave at Jaffa Gate? Where Can You Find a Neighborhood Oven to Use? What's on the Bridge Over the Way to the Western Wall? How to Get to Vienna Via the Old City? Why is the English Princess Buried in a Russian Church? The House Above the Floor of the Armenian Church. Where Did President Ben-Zvi Find a Quiet Spot? With Whom Did Richard Gere Share the "Fourth Wife's Room"? What Lies Shimmering at the Heart of the Museum? What's Special about Eliyahu's Pita Bread? What is Buddha Doing in a Suburbian House? Who Plays Bowls in the Middle of the Forest? Where Are the Indian Soldiers of His Majesty's Army Buried? What Lurks Near the Entrance to Hell? The Cistern that Became a Hamam, and the Hospital that Became a Hotel. How Much Honor Can the High Commissioner Bestow on the Cat? Who Warmed Themselves by the High Commissioner's Hearth? Is the Gate Crooked or Did the Floor Move? Who Built a White Bench by the Mar Elias Monastery? How Did the Concrete of the Gilo Security Wall become Transparent? Where Did the Animals Go When They Left Noah's Ark? Where Do the Stairs from the Mall Parking Lot Lead? A Work of Art Made to be Walked On. Where is the Brother of the Sundial on Jaffa Road? What Happens at Mahaneh Yehudah Market After the Vegetable Stall Owners Close for the Day? Where is the Entrance to the World's Most Secret Kabbalah Center? Where Did the Greek Patriarch, St. Simon, and Saul Tchernichowski Meet? How Far Were the Limbs of Og, the King of Bashan, Scattered? Where Can You Find Mohammad's Trusty Friend? The Secrets of the Armenian Garden of Eden. After Whom is Jimmy's Alley in the German Colony Named? **Who Taught Sir Moses Montefiore to Build the Flour Mill?** Who Dared Replace Jerusalem Stone With Tin Plating? The Oldest Villa in Rehavia. Where Are Prayers Translated into Paintings? The Synagogue Over the Catholic Chapel. What Happens When the Rabbi Dies in the Middle of the War? Who Lives Inside the Israel Museum?

The Anonymous Mill in Ratisbonne Yard

One of the ways Sir Moses Montefiore helped the Jews of Jerusalem was to put up a flour mill that would help them grind their flour more cheaply than using the services of the Arabs' mills. In 1860, he built the famous windmill at Mishkenot Shaananim.

While on a preliminary visit to Jerusalem to study the issue, he found that the city already had two such windmills. He described them thus: "I saw two other millstone houses, built there from new as I had heard. They bring a good livelihood to their two Greek owners."

One of the mills Montefiore describes no longer exists, but the other has been preserved. Back then, it stood in an empty field but, in 1877, the Ratisbonne Monastery was built around it, which protected it from the ravages of time and preserved its anonymity. Today, pedestrians and passing motorists cannot see it.

The mill and the Ratisbonne Monastery today sit in the heart of the Rehavia quarter. Despite its resemblance to the famous mill at Mishkenot Shaananim, next to the tall houses of the district, it is hard to distinguish its glorious past, and it is currently a residential building for Jerusalemites who like to live in exotic buildings.

The Ratisbonne Compound was built in 1877 by two converted Christian brothers from Strasburg, Theodor and Alfonse Ratisbonne, to help Jerusalem Jews who lived in abject poverty and to achieve a better understanding between Christians and Jews and even to convert Jews to Catholicism.

Passers-by are mostly familiar with the main façade facing Shmuel ha-Nagid Street which is designed in Renaissance style in perfect symmetry. Two arches connect the various wings of the building, and there is an entrance balcony as well as impressive steps leading to the entrance hall. The building also contains a chapel, bell tower, halls and study rooms (in certain periods, the building served as a school also attended by Jewish children). There are also service areas, such as kitchen and laundry room, rooms for monks, and dormitories for the students.

The rear of the building has a large yard, most of which is occupied by Rehavia houses but the small mill is still there. Its diminutive size and location raise the question of whether it ever actually served as a flour mill. In addition, the fact that the mill was there before the monastery also makes it difficult to properly identify it.

Some researchers believe that the round two-storied structure is a tower built by the Turks in the 1830s as part of a chain of towers used to transmit smoke signals between Jaffa and Jerusalem. Others claim it was a watch tower while there are those who believe this was a mill used by the monks at the monastery.

Either way, the authentic and well-preserved structure sits modestly behind the fancy well-appointed houses of Rehavia, still waiting for its true identity to be revealed.

The Ratisbonne Monastery yard, 24 Shmuel ha-Nagid Street, downtown Jerusalem.

Who Founded an African Village on the Roof of the Church of the Holy Sepulcher? What Do the Nuns Do at the Sixth Station? Is this a Synagogue or a Church? What Can You Find on the Second Floor of the Drapery Store? What's on Offer at Antioch's Descendants' Museum? Who is Really Buried in the Architects' Grave at Jaffa Gate? Where Can You Find a Neighborhood Oven to Use? What's on the Bridge Over the Way to the Western Wall? How to Get to Vienna Via the Old City? Why is the English Princess Buried in a Russian Church? The House Above the Floor of the Armenian Church. Where Did President Ben-Zvi Find a Quiet Spot? With Whom Did Richard Gere Share the "Fourth Wife's Room"? What Lies Shimmering at the Heart of the Museum? What's Special about Eliyahu's Pita Bread? What is Buddha Doing in a Suburbian House? Who Plays Bowls in the Middle of the Forest? Where Are the Indian Soldiers of His Majesty's Army Buried? What Lurks Near the Entrance to Hell? The Cistern that Became a Hamam, and the Hospital that Became a Hotel. How Much Honor Can the High Commissioner Bestow on the Cat? Who Warmed Themselves by the High Commissioner's Hearth? Is the Gate Crooked or Did the Floor Move? Who Built a White Bench by the Mar Elias Monastery? How Did the Concrete of the Gilo Security Wall become Transparent? Where Did the Animals Go When They Left Noah's Ark? Where Do the Stairs from the Mall Parking Lot Lead? A Work of Art Made to be Walked On. Where is the Brother of the Sundial on Jaffa Road? What Happens at Mahaneh Yehudah Market After the Vegetable Stall Owners Close for the Day? Where is the Entrance to the World's Most Secret Kabbalah Center? Where Did the Greek Patriarch, St. Simon, and Saul Tchernichowski Meet? How Far Were the Limbs of Og, the King of Bashan, Scattered? Where Can You Find Mohammad's Trusty Friend? The Secrets of the Armenian Garden of Eden. After Whom is Jimmy's Alley in the German Colony Named? Who Taught Sir Moses Montefiore to Build the Flour Mill? Who Dared Replace Jerusalem Stone With Tin Plating? The Oldest Villa in Rehavia. Where Are Prayers Translated into Paintings? The Synagogue Over the Catholic Chapel. What Happens When the Rabbi Dies in the Middle of the War? Who Lives Inside the Israel Museum?

The Last Vestiges of the Tin Plating Neighborhood

"Jerusalem of gold, of copper and tin" is the usual description of the Nahlaot district, an area of stone houses with red tiled roofs, winding streets, and picturesque alleys in the heart of Jerusalem.

No one who described the neighborhood, either in writing or paintings, described it as a neighborhood made of stone with tin plating, or tin-plated stone, or tin plating with bits of wood. In fact, there is so much tin plating here that the tin became synonymous with the place, and there are whole areas called tin districts.

The area called Nahlaot, in fact, comprises sixteen small neighborhoods in the heart of Jerusalem around Agrippas Street and Bezalel Street. Construction began there in 1875 as the sixth area outside the Old City walls after life within the walls became impossible due to overcrowding and poor sanitary conditions.

Initially, small neighborhoods sprang up – some built by philanthropists for the city's poor, some established by particular communities and there were *"kolel"* (community of people in the Land of Israel from a specific country or locality) neighborhoods built with donations sent from the *kolel* members' country of origin. Each neighborhood had its own character, and its own system of finances based on the organization responsible for setting it up.

Most of the neighborhoods in Nahlaot were built during the Ottoman Era. Neighborhoods were built close together, primarily to provide a sense of security, as they were isolated in the undeveloped expanses of new Jerusalem at the time. Another reason for their proximity was the wish of the Jews to adhere to the religious law of "the Sabbath domain."

Later, during the British Mandate period, Jerusalem experienced rapid development, during which many new neighborhoods were built with spacious apartments surrounded by gardens. Well-to-do families preferred to leave their homes in Nahlaot and relocate to the newer areas (Rehavia, Talpiyyot, Beit ha-Kerem, Kiryat Moshe). They left behind their poorer neighbors, the old and those who preferred the supportive environment of the older districts.

At the time, many Jews came to the Holy Land and, in particular, to Jerusalem. Europeans preferred the new green areas while many from eastern countries settled in Nahlaot which became a crowded poor area.

Residents were gradually forced to enlarge their apartments by adding extensions or enclosing balconies and rooms with simple cheap materials, such as tin and wood. Meanwhile, the cold, wet weather forced them to counter problems of dampness that seeped in through the stones. The cheap, quick solution was to put up an improvised casing of tin around the entire house, which created a "design" style that was unique to the area, incorporating grey tin with the yellowish Jerusalem stonework. The phenomenon became so widespread that the Shevet Tzedek neighborhood soon became known as the "tin neighborhood," and it is still known as such today.

The process of advanced deterioration is generally irreversible. At the same time, however, in the 1970s an opposite trend began to emerge, beginning with the arrival of young students drawn there by the charm of the old neighborhoods and the old houses. The students were followed by people with means looking to realize the potential of the old stone houses. They developed the yards and balconies, renovated the steps, fixed leaks, removed the makeshift additions and turned the neighborhood into a beautiful and spacious area.

Nevertheless, the tin houses have not disappeared entirely. Many were renovated during the preservation process and some now look like the work of an artist rather than the result of improvisation. And so, thanks to people who respect old buildings, a historical Jerusalem phenomenon called the tin districts has survived.

The Shevet Tzedek neighborhood in Nahlaot.

Who Founded an African Village on the Roof of the Church of the Holy Sepulcher? What Do the Nuns Do at the Sixth Station? Is this a Synagogue or a Church? What Can You Find on the Second Floor of the Drapery Store? What's on Offer at Antioch's Descendants' Museum? Who is Really Buried in the Architects' Grave at Jaffa Gate? Where Can You Find a Neighborhood Oven to Use? What's on the Bridge Over the Way to the Western Wall? How to Get to Vienna Via the Old City? Why is the English Princess Buried in a Russian Church? The House Above the Floor of the Armenian Church. Where Did President Ben-Zvi Find a Quiet Spot? With Whom Did Richard Gere Share the "Fourth Wife's Room"? What Lies Shimmering at the Heart of the Museum? What's Special about Eliyahu's Pita Bread? What is Buddha Doing in a Suburban House? Who Plays Bowls in the Middle of the Forest? Where Are the Indian Soldiers of His Majesty's Army Buried? What Lurks Near the Entrance to Hell? The Cistern that Became a Hamam, and the Hospital that Became a Hotel. How Much Honor Can the High Commissioner Bestow on the Cat? Who Warmed Themselves by the High Commissioner's Hearth? Is the Gate Crooked or Did the Floor Move? Who Built a White Bench by the Mar Elias Monastery? How Did the Concrete of the Gilo Security Wall become Transparent? Where Did the Animals Go When They Left Noah's Ark? Where Do the Stairs from the Mall Parking Lot Lead? A Work of Art Made to be Walked On. Where is the Brother of the Sundial on Jaffa Road? What Happens at Mahaneh Yehudah Market After the Vegetable Stall Owners Close for the Day? Where is the Entrance to the World's Most Secret Kabbalah Center? Where Did the Greek Patriarch, St. Simon, and Saul Tchernichowski Meet? How Far Were the Limbs of Og, the King of Bashan, Scattered? Where Can You Find Mohammad's Trusty Friend? The Secrets of the Armenian Garden of Eden. After Whom is Jimmy's Alley in the German Colony Named? Who Taught Sir Moses Montefiore to Build the Flour Mill? Who Dared Replace Jerusalem Stone With Tin Plating? **The Oldest Villa in Rehavia.** Where Are Prayers Translated into Paintings? The Synagogue Over the Catholic Chapel. What Happens When the Rabbi Dies in the Middle of the War? Who Lives Inside the Israel Museum?

Jason's Tomb on Alfasi Street

"The district of Rehavia is well known and, nonetheless, contains secret places which few know about. There is a wide street in Rehavia with a tomb in the middle of it; a majestic and carved tomb, Jason's Tomb, a priest from the days of the Second Temple."

Thus, in his book *The Truth Shall Spring Forth from the Earth*, writer Haim Sabato describes the tomb between two beautiful houses on Alfasi Street in the neighborhood of Rehavia.

The phenomenon of discovering tombs every time a new road is built in Jerusalem is well known, however Jason's Tomb, discovered in 1956 during the construction of a house there, is one of the most extraordinary.

The tomb, which was discovered in its entirety, is so majestic and impressive that it is in no way inferior to the houses on either side of it, at Nos. 8 and 10, Alfasi Street. It is surrounded by a neat garden – as well tended as the gardens of the nearby homes – like the houses, it is made with Jerusalem stone and reflects the splendor and sumptuousness of the district.

The tomb was discovered by chance during preparation work for the construction of a house. The excavators discovered a burial cave and called it Jason's Tomb, in accordance with the name in the Hebrew inscription engraved on the side of the cave. The burial cave probably dates from the Hellenistic era, from the time of the Hasmoneans, and it was used up to the time of King Herod. It is fronted by three yards connected by an arch and topped by a restored pyramid, which imparts an appearance of an elegant house.

The walls of the entrance room are decorated with a seven-branched candelabrum, charcoal paintings of a battleship pursuing a merchant ship and a painting of a crouching deer. Aramaic and Greek inscriptions were also discovered, including a lamentation about Jason's death. The front of the cave, whose walls are lined with plaster, has a single column with two rooms hewn on the other side. The left room has burial recesses, and bones were discovered in the other room. Both rooms were closed off by stone blocks that were matched to the shape of the entrance. The blocks were discovered near by.

It is hard to distinguish the structure as a tomb, either because of the aesthetic qualities of the tomb itself or the houses around it. You have to take several walks up and down the street, however, before you fully realize that the structure, which fits in with the houses so well, is in fact a tomb.

Alfasi Street, Rehavia.

Who Founded an African Village on the Roof of the Church of the Holy Sepulcher? What Do the Nuns Do at the Sixth Station? Is this a Synagogue or a Church? What Can You Find on the Second Floor of the Drapery Store? What's on Offer at Antioch's Descendants' Museum? Who is Really Buried in the Architects' Grave at Jaffa Gate? Where Can You Find a Neighborhood Oven to Use? What's on the Bridge Over the Way to the Western Wall? How to Get to Vienna Via the Old City? Why is the English Princess Buried in a Russian Church? The House Above the Floor of the Armenian Church. Where Did President Ben-Zvi Find a Quiet Spot? With Whom Did Richard Gere Share the "Fourth Wife's Room"? What Lies Shimmering at the Heart of the Museum? What's Special about Eliyahu's Pita Bread? What is Buddha Doing in a Suburbian House? Who Plays Bowls in the Middle of the Forest? Where Are the Indian Soldiers of His Majesty's Army Buried? What Lurks Near the Entrance to Hell? The Cistern that Became a Hamam, and the Hospital that Became a Hotel. How Much Honor Can the High Commissioner Bestow on the Cat? Who Warmed Themselves by the High Commissioner's Hearth? Is the Gate Crooked or Did the Floor Move? Who Built a White Bench by the Mar Elias Monastery? How Did the Concrete of the Gilo Security Wall become Transparent? Where Did the Animals Go When They Left Noah's Ark? Where Do the Stairs from the Mall Parking Lot Lead? A Work of Art Made to be Walked On. Where is the Brother of the Sundial on Jaffa Road? What Happens at Mahaneh Yehudah Market After the Vegetable Stall Owners Close for the Day? Where is the Entrance to the World's Most Secret Kabbalah Center? Where Did the Greek Patriarch, St. Simon, and Saul Tchernichowski Meet? How Far Were the Limbs of Og, the King of Bashan, Scattered? Where Can You Find Mohammad's Trusty Friend? The Secrets of the Armenian Garden of Eden. After Whom is Jimmy's Alley in the German Colony Named? Who Taught Sir Moses Montefiore to Build the Flour Mill? Who Dared Replace Jerusalem Stone With Tin Plating? The Oldest Villa in Rehavia. Where Are Prayers Translated into Paintings? The Synagogue Over the Catholic Chapel. What Happens When the Rabbi Dies in the Middle of the War? Who Lives Inside the Israel Museum?

The Psalms Museum in Rabbi Kook's House

There are 150 chapters in the Book of Psalms, and there are 150 paintings in the Psalms Museum – one for each psalm.

The Psalms Museum, small, cozy and not too well known, is located in none other than the home of the late Chief Rabbi of Israel, Rabbi Abraham Isaac Kook, of blessed memory, on Rabbi Kook Street in Jerusalem. This is the museum of a single person, artist Moshe Zvi Berger, who dedicated 15 years of his life to painting each of the chapters of the Book of Psalms.

Berger is a graduate of some of the world's top art schools and has exhibited works in many museums. A number of his works is even included in the private collection of the Lubavitcher Rebbe. After producing giant murals across the United States, Berger finally found his vocation. He sees himself as an instrument for converting sacred texts from an intellectual process of hearing – prayers are spoken and heard – to a process of seeing, as paintings. In painting, he translated the 150 psalms into a visual medium of painting and gave them a contemporary look, making them more palatable for a generation used to learning through vision.

Berger does not mean to change the Scriptures, the words or the sense, by adding to them, reducing or changing them. He wants to create the possibility of experiencing them through figures and colors.

It is not common for a religious, even ultra-orthodox, person to work in the arts but Berger does not consider himself something out of the ordinary. His art is based on knowledge and study, and he draws his ideas from the Kabbalah and from the Book of the Zohar. Translating the psalms from poetry to visual images is a tough challenge. After studying the meaning of the psalms, the artist chose a single verse from each chapter and interpreted it in painting, with colors, lines and representation that reflected the sense of the verse, focusing on beauty and balance.

Berger found it difficult to maintain a style for all 150 chapters of the Book of Psalms. Each painting is different, as each chapter is different. As Berger related to all his paintings as a single work, he felt committed to maintaining the style he chose so as not to harm the uniformity of the entire work.

The same colors appear in the large works exhibited in the museum's halls. The same colors are carefully repeated – gleaming, bright, and optimistic. This is not done by chance, as the painting technique was chosen in advance to facilitate the mixing of the acrylic transparent paints, and the transition from color to color.

The artist allowed himself freedom in choosing the painting technique, but not in the choice of colors. Here, he based his selection on Kabbalistic texts and the Book of the Zohar according to which the colors allude to the highest roots of the supernatural.

Berger used only seven colors – the seven colors of the rainbow – in the hope that these colors would allow the transition of forces from above. He believed that the visible colors – despite being material – are able to impact the spiritual dimension.

There is a lot of light in the paintings, and an abundance of beauty in the small museum. The elderly painter is a religious man but, above all, he is an aesthete. These aesthetics are present in every aspect of his life, from his deepest religious beliefs, and his intellectual and learned beliefs, to the design of this small museum – in the decoration of the ceilings with colors that match the paintings, in forgoing the arrangement of the paintings according to the order of the chapters in the Book of Psalms, and in placing the paintings to: "create harmony and uplift the spirit."

Rabbi Kooks House, Ha-Rav Kook Street, Jerusalem.

Who Founded an African Village on the Roof of the Church of the Holy Sepulcher? What Do the Nuns Do at the Sixth Station? Is this a Synagogue or a Church? What Can You Find on the Second Floor of the Drapery Store? What's on Offer at Antioch's Descendants' Museum? Who is Really Buried in the Architects' Grave at Jaffa Gate? Where Can You Find a Neighborhood Oven to Use? What's on the Bridge Over the Way to the Western Wall? How to Get to Vienna Via the Old City? Why is the English Princess Buried in a Russian Church? The House Above the Floor of the Armenian Church. Where Did President Ben-Zvi Find a Quiet Spot? With Whom Did Richard Gere Share the "Fourth Wife's Room"? What Lies Shimmering at the Heart of the Museum? What's Special about Eliyahu's Pita Bread? What is Buddha Doing in a Suburbian House? Who Plays Bowls in the Middle of the Forest? Where Are the Indian Soldiers of His Majesty's Army Buried? What Lurks Near the Entrance to Hell? The Cistern that Became a Hamam, and the Hospital that Became a Hotel. How Much Honor Can the High Commissioner Bestow on the Cat? Who Warmed Themselves by the High Commissioner's Hearth? Is the Gate Crooked or Did the Floor Move? Who Built a White Bench by the Mar Elias Monastery? How Did the Concrete of the Gilo Security Wall become Transparent? Where Did the Animals Go When They Left Noah's Ark? Where Do the Stairs from the Mall Parking Lot Lead? A Work of Art Made to be Walked On. Where is the Brother of the Sundial on Jaffa Road? What Happens at Mahaneh Yehudah Market After the Vegetable Stall Owners Close for the Day? Where is the Entrance to the World's Most Secret Kabbalah Center? Where Did the Greek Patriarch, St. Simon, and Saul Tchernichowski Meet? How Far Were the Limbs of Og, the King of Bashan, Scattered? Where Can You Find Mohammad's Trusty Friend? The Secrets of the Armenian Garden of Eden. After Whom is Jimmy's Alley in the German Colony Named? Who Taught Sir Moses Montefiore to Build the Flour Mill? Who Dared Replace Jerusalem Stone With Tin Plating? The Oldest Villa in Rehavia. Where Are Prayers Translated into Paintings? **The Synagogue Over the Catholic Chapel.** What Happens When the Rabbi Dies in the Middle of the War? Who Lives Inside the Israel Museum?

The Ancient Synagogue that Was Brought from Italy to Hillel Street

Only in a city like Jerusalem can you find an Italian synagogue over a Catholic chapel in a place called the German Compound.

The synagogue, located on Hillel Street in the center of the city, is an old beautiful stone building designed with Renaissance-style symmetry, a neo-Gothic façade, and windows with pointed Gothic arches and carved ornamentation.

The Italian synagogue was moved in 1952, in its entirety, to Jerusalem from the town of Conegliano, in the Italian region of Veneto, near Venice. Consecrated in Conegliano in 1701, it was used by the Jewish community there up to the beginning of the twentieth century. The last prayers were recited there during the High Holidays of 1918, and even that was by chance, since it came about as a result of the occupation of northern Italy by the Austro-Hungarian army, and an army rabbi by the name of Harry Deutsch who was looking for a place to hold prayers for himself and Jewish soldiers.

The rabbi's quest led him to an elderly woman who presented herself as the only Jew left in the town. She said she had the key to the synagogue that had been abandoned. Throughout the High Holidays, the synagogue played host to the rabbi and the Jewish soldiers. After the hostilities ended, and the Austrian army withdrew, the synagogue doors were shut again and were only reopened in Jerusalem in 1952.

A group of immigrants from Italy, headed by Rabbi Dr. Menahem Hartam and Moshe ha-Cohen Pirani, decided to move the synagogue to Jerusalem, where, they said, prayers would once again be heard within its walls.

The synagogue was consecrated with a sumptuous ceremony in the presence of many Italian-born Jews and other guests, including one ultra-orthodox Jew dressed in black garments and a wide-brimmed hat. He had a white beard and long side locks. The man aroused much interest and, when he was asked as to his identity, said his name was Harry Deutsch and that he was once the Chief Rabbi of the Austrian army. He was also the last

The ancient synagogue on the second floor, over a catholic chapel, in a building that was built by German pilgrims

person to have prayed in the original synagogue in Conegliano. Judging by his amazement, one can conclude that the restored synagogue was very similar to the original.

Here, too, as in Italy, the synagogue is located on the second floor of an old building, although the hall in Jerusalem is somewhat larger than the original, and a little lower. Just like then, the Torah ark today is in the eastern wall of the synagogue, and the *tevah (bimah)* is inside a recess of the western wall, resembling a small theater stage surrounded by curtains around the entrance.

The worshipers' seats rested against the north wall and the south wall of the hall, and were covered by Venetian-style wood. The women's section surrounded the entire hall, and seating arrangements there were similar to those in the men's section. Although the women were obscured by carved, fashioned wooden beams, the women could move them to one side during prayers, as they wished. The seating arrangement allowed room for ceremonial rituals, processions with the Torah scrolls, concerts, and even dances.

However, the old stone building in Jerusalem served as a religious compound not only for Jews but for Catholics too. The synagogue is located right on top of a Christian chapel.

The Germans built the chapel structure in 1886 as a hospice for pilgrims visiting the Holy City and as a school for Syrian girls. It was called The German Catholic Institution in front of the Jaffa Gate. The chapel is located inside a vaulted room on the ground floor, and its walls are decorated with Christian religious motifs and religious verses. It was decorated by a pilgrim painter who paid for his accommodation at the hospice with his work.

After a while, it was discovered that the institution was too far away from Jaffa Gate and the Old City and, thus, could not serve the pilgrims or the students in the Old City. It was transferred to a large building opposite the Damascus Gate. The old building on Hillel Street went through numerous changes until it became a hostel for the old synagogue from Conegliano, and today serves as the synagogue for the city's Italian community, whose numbers increased tenfold over the Conegliano community. The place is very active, with prayers held every Friday and Saturday, as well

The catholic chapel over which stands the Italian synagogue

as on religious holidays, and also hosts events like weddings and bar mitzvas.

The chapel and synagogue have a good neighborly relationship, without each trying to "convert" the other. The chapel's authenticity is preserved and restored, serving visitors to the synagogue for different events without harming its character and style.

27 Hillel Street, downtown Jerusalem.

Who Founded an African Village on the Roof of the Church of the Holy Sepulcher? What Do the Nuns Do at the Sixth Station? Is this a Synagogue or a Church? What Can You Find on the Second Floor of the Drapery Store? What's on Offer at Antioch's Descendants' Museum? Who is Really Buried in the Architects' Grave at Jaffa Gate? Where Can You Find a Neighborhood Oven to Use? What's on the Bridge Over the Way to the Western Wall? How to Get to Vienna Via the Old City? Why is the English Princess Buried in a Russian Church? The House Above the Floor of the Armenian Church. Where Did President Ben-Zvi Find a Quiet Spot? With Whom Did Richard Gere Share the "Fourth Wife's Room"? What Lies Shimmering at the Heart of the Museum? What's Special about Eliyahu's Pita Bread? What is Buddha Doing in a Suburbian House? Who Plays Bowls in the Middle of the Forest? Where Are the Indian Soldiers of His Majesty's Army Buried? What Lurks Near the Entrance to Hell? The Cistern that Became a Hamam, and the Hospital that Became a Hotel. How Much Honor Can the High Commissioner Bestow on the Cat? Who Warmed Themselves by the High Commissioner's Hearth? Is the Gate Crooked or Did the Floor Move? Who Built a White Bench by the Mar Elias Monastery? How Did the Concrete of the Gilo Security Wall become Transparent? Where Did the Animals Go When They Left Noah's Ark? Where Do the Stairs from the Mall Parking Lot Lead? A Work of Art Made to be Walked On. Where is the Brother of the Sundial on Jaffa Road? What Happens at Mahaneh Yehudah Market After the Vegetable Stall Owners Close for the Day? Where is the Entrance to the World's Most Secret Kabbalah Center? Where Did the Greek Patriarch, St. Simon, and Saul Tchernichowski Meet? How Far Were the Limbs of Og, the King of Bashan, Scattered? Where Can You Find Mohammad's Trusty Friend? The Secrets of the Armenian Garden of Eden. After Whom is Jimmy's Alley in the German Colony Named? Who Taught Sir Moses Montefiore to Build the Flour Mill? Who Dared Replace Jerusalem Stone With Tin Plating? The Oldest Villa in Rehavia. Where Are Prayers Translated into Paintings? The Synagogue Over the Catholic Chapel. What Happens When the Rabbi Dies in the Middle of the War? Who Lives Inside the Israel Museum?

The Grave of the Gerer Rebbe on Jaffa Road

There are two graves on Jaffa Road, opposite the entrance to the Mahaneh Yehuda market, near the opening of the narrow Schwartz Alley. The graves are strange looking as they have no headstones, only an enormous amount of stones piled up on top of them, as per Jewish custom. In view of the modest surroundings, it is surprising to discover that these are the graves of two Chief Rabbis from the grand Hassidic community from Gur.

Why were two rabbis from one of the Hassidic world's leading communities buried at the entrance of an anonymous alley rather than on the Mount of Olives? It seems that, not only in life, but also in death, it is all a matter of timing.

The first rabbi to be buried here was Rabbi Abraham Mordechai Alter, who was known as "Imrei Emet" (sayings of truth), heir to a dynasty of great rabbis founded in 1860 in the town of Gora-Kalwaria in Poland. The founding father was Rabbi Isaac Meir or, as he was known, "Hiddushei ha-Rim" (ha-Rim innovations) which is the title of his famous book. After his death, his grandson Rabbi Judah Leib, known as "Sefat Emet" (the Language of Truth) – the title of his book – took his place. During his term as leader the Gur community grew considerably, but he died at the age of 58 and his son, Rabbi Abraham Mordehai of Gur, inherited his position and it was he who founded a center for the community in Jerusalem in the early 1920s.

He first came to Jerusalem in 1921, after he had been greatly impressed by the Balfour Declaration. Here, he met High Commissioner Herbert Samuel, Rabbi Kook and other important figures. It was during this visit that he decided to purchase some land and establish a center for his community. Immediately after the acquisition, large numbers of Hassidim moved to Jerusalem and established the Gur community in the city. The Rabbi of Gur visited Jerusalem five times but never settled there, each time returning to his community in Poland.

With the outbreak of World War II, he moved to Warsaw and stayed there until the Nazi occupation. Somehow his Hassidim managed to help him escape the Nazis, and he eventually arrived

ailing in Jerusalem, in 1940, settling at the Sefat Emet Yeshiva (Talmudic College).

The rabbi died in 1948, in the middle of the War of Independence. Jerusalem was being bombarded and was under siege. The rabbi's family appealed to the Red Cross to allow his body to be moved to the Mount of Olives. When their application remained unheeded, however, they had no choice but to bury him near the room where he had lived close to his death. The grave was dug in the yard and, at the end of the war, his son Rabbi Israel Alter decided to leave the grave in its place.

The two sons of Imrei Emet, who succeeded him as leaders of the community, were buried on the Mount of Olives. The third brother, Rabbi Pinhas Menachem, became leader of the community in 1992, following the death of his brother Simha Bunim Alter, and served as leader until his death, just three and a half years later. He died suddenly in 1996 and was buried in the yard near his father.

As such, the temporary burial place became an important and holy site for Gur Hassidim. But not just for them. Many visit the spot to make pleas and leave supplicatory slips of paper there. There are stories, among the Hassidim, of miracles that have occurred, of sick people who have been cured, and of barren women who have subsequently given birth.

The yard was recently added to with a strange looking red brick "structure." Its color strikingly contrasted with the Jerusalem stone of the other buildings in the area and, although there are windows and doors in it, this is not an actual building, only a wall. Moreover, despite its height, on closer inspection it transpires that this is, in fact, a miniature.

The wall is a scaled-down version of the front of the *beit midrash* (study room) of the Gur Hassidic community in the town of Gora-Kalwaria in Poland, which served as the community's center until the outbreak of World War II. The wall in Jerusalem is about half the size of the original wall and was built based on old photographs as well as the memories of the Hassidim who survived the Holocaust and came to Jerusalem. The model was placed near the two graves and has turned the spot into a sort of improvised burial estate which is, nonetheless, holy to many people.

Schwartz Alley, opposite the main entrance to the Mahaneh Yehuda market.

Who Founded an African Village on the Roof of the Church of the Holy Sepulcher? What Do the Nuns Do at the Sixth Station? Is this a Synagogue or a Church? What Can You Find on the Second Floor of the Drapery Store? What's on Offer at Antioch's Descendants' Museum? Who is Really Buried in the Architects' Grave at Jaffa Gate? Where Can You Find a Neighborhood Oven to Use? What's on the Bridge Over the Way to the Western Wall? How to Get to Vienna Via the Old City? Why is the English Princess Buried in a Russian Church? The House Above the Floor of the Armenian Church. Where Did President Ben-Zvi Find a Quiet Spot? With Whom Did Richard Gere Share the "Fourth Wife's Room"? What Lies Shimmering at the Heart of the Museum? What's Special about Eliyahu's Pita Bread? What is Buddha Doing in a Suburbian House? Who Plays Bowls in the Middle of the Forest? Where Are the Indian Soldiers of His Majesty's Army Buried? What Lurks Near the Entrance to Hell? The Cistern that Became a Hamam, and the Hospital that Became a Hotel. How Much Honor Can the High Commissioner Bestow on the Cat? Who Warmed Themselves by the High Commissioner's Hearth? Is the Gate Crooked or Did the Floor Move? Who Built a White Bench by the Mar Elias Monastery? How Did the Concrete of the Gilo Security Wall become Transparent? Where Did the Animals Go When They Left Noah's Ark? Where Do the Stairs from the Mall Parking Lot Lead? A Work of Art Made to be Walked On. Where is the Brother of the Sundial on Jaffa Road? What Happens at Mahaneh Yehudah Market After the Vegetable Stall Owners Close for the Day? Where is the Entrance to the World's Most Secret Kabbalah Center? Where Did the Greek Patriarch, St. Simon, and Saul Tchernichowski Meet? How Far Were the Limbs of Og, the King of Bashan, Scattered? Where Can You Find Mohammad's Trusty Friend? The Secrets of the Armenian Garden of Eden. After Whom is Jimmy's Alley in the German Colony Named? Who Taught Sir Moses Montefiore to Build the Flour Mill? Who Dared Replace Jerusalem Stone With Tin Plating? The Oldest Villa in Rehavia. Where Are Prayers Translated into Paintings? The Synagogue Over the Catholic Chapel. What Happens When the Rabbi Dies in the Middle of the War? Who Lives Inside the Israel Museum?

Mrs. Bergman's Will

Deep inside the Israel Museum, right behind the Youth Wing, is a house. It looks just like the museum building and appears to be an integral part of it, as if it is just another museum wing. It has the same external large white stone covering, the same style of windows, and the same flat roof. There is no perceptible difference at all.

Until recently, the house was occupied by an elderly lady, a famous art collector and a staunch Zionist. Her name was Charlotte Bergman. But, why did she choose to live inside the museum? How did she live there among the hubbub of the visitors during the day, and with the repressive loneliness that descended on the place after closing hours?

When the museum was officially opened in 1965, it wasn't at all clear whether the museum would be able to attract important works of art. Israel, in those days, was not skilled in importing significant collections. The museum's founders did not know if collectors with large holdings would be willing to come all the way to Jerusalem to display the works of art that they had labored too hard to acquire.

In fact, many collectors were concerned that the museum that was gradually emerging in a far off city was not sufficiently attractive for their works of art. Mrs. Bergman thought otherwise. She was an English-born American widow with an impressive art collection she had built up together with her husband Lewis who died in 1955.

Mrs. Bergman responded to the Zionist challenge with enthusiasm, but she had one condition – she would live together with her collection, inside the museum. As the founders of the museum considered her collection adequately important, they agreed to her precondition with alacrity.

The Bergman collection included sculptures and paintings by Henry Moore, whom the couple came to know personally, after Charlotte bought a Moore painting in a frame store in London, where she had her paintings framed, for the ridiculously cheap price of twenty seven and a half shillings – just over a pound. She subsequently bought another Moore painting at the same shop, and then asked to meet him as she believed he was a great artist.

Besides the Moore works, the collection also includes works by Bracques, Maillot, and Picasso as well as works by lesser known artists in whom the collector believed and whose works she acquired.

Prior to Mrs. Bergman's move, it was agreed that she would finance the construction work of her new home. It would be built in the same style as the museum, and would be erected by the same professionals who were building the museum itself. For the collector, construction of the house was no simple matter. The museum staff, the architects, and the builders were not experienced in buildings houses for people of Charlotte Bergman's standing, and they encountered quite a few problems in drawing up the agreement with her. For example, she wanted to bring her grand piano with her to Jerusalem. The builders were not adept at dealing with the dimensions of the piano, and the entrances to the house were not big enough. Not only that, she brought with her gold taps which the Jerusalem plumbers had never encountered before. Who, in Jerusalem of 1965, had ever heard of gold taps?

But, in the end, the house was completed. It is a single-story building overlooking Emek ha-Matzleva (the Valley of the Cross). Its rooms are full of works of art. The music room has a large expensive painting by Bracques alongside a Chagall painting. The bedroom contains works by Henry Moore, and the living room has a giant painting by a Japanese artist. There is also a room devoted to ceramic works by Picasso, and there are also two sketches by him there.

Mrs. Bergman may have lived among her works of art, as she so wanted, but it is not clear how much fun it was for her to be there at night, when the place was deserted. She liked to have guests over, and she showed off her collection to art-loving Jerusalemites. She also held concerts there, and cultural evenings, which could only be held in a large house, of which there are few in Jerusalem.

According to the agreement between Mrs. Bergman and the museum, she was at liberty to live in the house with her works for her lifetime. After her death, ownership of the house was transferred to the museum. The museum may not change anything in the house, but must preserve it as is, and open it up to visitors to show them how the art collector lived. She also insisted that no one else should live in the house.

Mrs. Bergman lived in the house from 1967 to 2002. She died at the age of 99. Since then, the museum has endeavored to honor her will. The house looks like it is still inhabited, and the works of art are still in their original positions. However, the museum is struggling to open it up to the general public as Mrs. Bergman asked that no partitions be placed between the public and the works of art, and this is hard to put into practice.

It is hard to prevent visitors from touching the paintings, the lighting there is unsuitable for displaying the valuable works and, in the dining room, the watercolors on the walls are fading due to the strong sunlight that floods in through the windows and, as a result, the blinds have been drawn. This makes viewing the pictures impossible. At this stage, the house is not open to the public but only to select organized parties.

The Israel Museum compound, Ruppin Boulevard.

206

Acknowledgements

To everyone who revealed the "secrets" to me, some of whom did not know me but, nonetheless, expressed a great willingness to help, out of respect for writing and books:

Bezalel Amikam, my friend, who accompanied me anywhere I wanted
Mrs. Aliza Olmert
Mayor of Jerusalem, Mr. Uri Lupolianski, who told me about the grave
  of the Gerer Rebbe
Dr. Doron Barr
Renee Guttman
Lee Berlman
Ezra Corman
Shlomi Shahal
Balfour Hakkak
Yossi Koren, who taught me the excitement of making discoveries
And my friends Ronnie Kodinski-Yizhar and Efrat Peled, who devoted
  themselves to the task as if it were their own, and dedicated their
  time and their soul.

In writing this book I was helped by many books (all in Hebrew) lovingly dedicated to Jerusalem:

Architecture in Jerusalem, Construction in the Old City
David Kroyanker; Keter Publishing, 1993

The New Guide to Israel – Jerusalem
Sefi Ben-Yosef, (ed.); Keter Publishing, Ministry of Defense Publishing House 2001

The Guide to Israel – A Practical Encyclopedia about Israel
Aryeh Yitzhaki (ed.); Keter Publishing, Ministry of Defense Publishing House, 1978

Districts of Jerusalem – The Story of the Construction and Development of Jerusalem outside the Walls
Jacob Gellis; Sefarim Rishonim, 5733 (1972–73)

The City of Rest – Cemeteries in Jerusalem
Meron Benvenishti; Keter Publishing, 1990

The Hill of Dispute – The Struggle for the Temple Mount, Jews and Moslems, Religion and Politics
Nadav Shragai; Keter Publishing, 1995

Jerusalem and All Its Paths
Eyal Meron (ed.); Yitzhak Ben-Zvi Memorial Publishing, 1996

Jerusalem, The New City
Ze'ev Vilnai; Ahiever Publishing, 1974

Ariel – An Encyclopedia of the Land of Israel
Ze'ev Vilnai; Am Oved Publishing, 1984

The Vilnai Encyclopedia of Jerusalem
Ze'ev Vilnai; Ahiever Publishing, 1993

Nahlaot in the Heart of the City
Nirit Shalev-Kaliffa; Yitzhak Ben-Zvi Memorial Publishing, 2003

Kadmoniot 26
Israel Exploration Society Publishing, 1993